BELIEF, UNBELIEF, ETHICS AND LIFE

Also by Leslie Scrase:

Days in the Sun (children's stories, with Jean Head)
In Travellings Often
Booklet on Anglican/Methodist Conversations
Some Sussex and Surrey Scrases
Diamond Parents
The Sunlight Glances Through (poetry)
Some Ancestors of Humanism
An Evacuee
Conversations (on Matthew's Gospel)
        between an Atheist and a Christian
A Prized Pupil!
A Reluctant Seaman
The Game Goes On (poetry)
It's Another World
A Talented Bureaucrat
Town Mouse and Country Mouse (nature diary)
More from the Country Mouse (nature diary)
Kenneth and Bob (children's story)
Coping With Death
Letting off Steam (short essays)
Scribblings of an old romantic (poems)
Happy Endings (short stories)
An Unbeliever's Guide to the Bible
The Four Gospels Through an Outside Window
        – A Commentary

BELIEF, UNBELIEF, ETHICS & LIFE

LESLIE SCRASE

UNITED WRITERS
Cornwall

UNITED WRITERS PUBLICATIONS LTD
Ailsa, Castle Gate, Penzance, Cornwall.
www.unitedwriters.co.uk

British Library Cataloguing in Publication Data:
A catalogue record for this book is
available from the British Library.

ISBN 9781852001650

Printed and bound in Great Britain by
United Writers Publications Ltd.,
Cornwall.

To my children:
Richard, Andrew, Jean and Christine.

Acknowledgements

A proper academic quotes sources, litters pages with footnotes, and perhaps far too rarely goes beyond sources to express a personal opinion! I'm afraid I've always been the reverse (far too cocky and big headed?). I have needed to chew over my sources until I could either make them my own or discard them, which makes proper acknowledgements impossible.

This study began in my student days when I was indebted to an excellent bunch of tutors: Bertram Clogg, Harold Roberts, Gordon Rupp, Clive Thexton, I don't remember his first name Goldhawk, David Head and Amos Creswell.

Many of our textbooks were also well worth study. Between our lectures and the textbooks I built up a copious stock of notes. The notes for this book swelled until they overfilled a box-file – a pile of stuff I've now been able to throw away! I no longer have even the names of the books on which my studies were first built. Was one of them by Trevor Nunn? So the following bibliography is hopelessly inadequate:

James Thrower, *The Alternative Tradition* (Mouton)
Gopalan, *Outline of Jainism* (Wiley Eastern Private Ltd)
K.M. Sen, *Hinduism* (Penguin)
G. Humphreys, *Buddhism* (Penguin)
D.C.Lau, *The Analects of Confucius* (Penguin)
D.C.Lau, *The Lao Tzu* (Penguin)
Bouquet, *Ancient or World Religions*
Sir R.W. Livingstone, *Greek Ideals and Modern Life*
Bertrand Russell, *History of Western Philosophy* (Unwin)
Dorothea Wender, *Hesiod and Theognis* (Penguin)
E.V. Rieu, *Homer's Iliad and Odyssey* (Penguin)
H.D.F. Kitto, *The Greeks* (Pelican)
Thucydides trans. Warner, *The Pelopponesian War* (Penguin)
H.J. Blackham, *Humanism* – revised edition (Harvester)
W.H.S. Jones and Dr E.T. Withington
        some of The Loeb Classics (Heinemann)
Aristotle's Ethics (Penguin)
Lucretius, *The Nature of the Universe* (Penguin)
Epicurus, *A Guide to Happiness* (Phoenix)
David B. Barrett. *Sects, cults and Alternative Religions*
Thomas Merton, *The Way of Chuang Tzu* (Shambala)
Nehru, *The Discovery of India*

Among the books I have used are two of my own! *Some Ancestors of Humanism* (South Place Ethical Society) now out of print, and *Coping with Death* – 3rd edition (United Writers).

Of *Ancestors* Jim Herrick wrote: 'No one can fail to be enlightened by his lively account and led to delve further into this fascinating strand of humanist history.'

If somewhere, someone felt the same about this book, I would be more than content.

Finally, it is impossible for me to express my gratitude to Malcolm Sheppard or my indebtedness to him. Through United Writers Publications, he has edited and published my work for almost twenty years – always with kindness and generosity and immaculate efficiency. In my own experience he has been quite simply, the best.

Contents

Preface

Not long ago I watched Howard Goodall's story of music on television and thoroughly enjoyed it. He prefaced every programme by stressing that this was his own story of music and that others would have told the story in a different way.

Although I love music my knowledge is pretty limited. But in spite of that, from time to time I found myself (in my head) pointing out that his story was only the story of European (and later American) music. And there was also an occasional, 'Hey, what about. . ?' or 'Why didn't you. . ?' or even, 'Hm, I'm not so sure about that.'

Part of me wishes that my book could reach as large an audience as he reached! But I would want to stress that this is *my own* (perhaps highly idiosyncratic) story of religion, unbelief, ethics and life.

I'm quite sure that any reader will frequently be saying, 'Hey, what about. . ?' or 'Why didn't you. . ?' or 'Hm, I'm not so sure about that,' or things that are a good deal less polite.

If you do, then look at the story for yourselves – preferably even more thoroughly and carefully than I have done. And then create your own story.

In a sense, I have whittled over these things all my life yet I am still not sure how important they are. Some of my grandchildren are studying philosophy and ethics for their A levels. I wonder what they will make of their studies or whether they will understand any better than I did.

To students and practitioners of religions, philosophies and codes of ethics, these things are all crucially important. They are also important to rulers and politicians as they try to keep ordinary people in line.

But when we are living our lives as they should be lived, we don't have to think about how they should be lived. There is no need to *think* about how they should be lived. Most people are honest and righteous without realising it. They are trustworthy without people telling them that they must be. They are reliable without anyone needing them to clock in and clock out. They are always ready to help one another and never think of themselves as generous or kind. They love one another without ever needing a law to tell them that they must. They are the foundation of all human society; the ones who really deserve to be called 'the salt of the earth'.

So is there any value in anything that I have written? As usual, I have written because I needed to get these things out of my system. Having done so, I can safely leave it to any readers I manage to find to judge whether it has been worthwhile. Of one of my previous books a reviewer wrote: 'Leslie needs to go out to the theatre more or to dinner. . .'!

There is plenty of theatre in my memory bank but we

rarely venture out nowadays after dark. And with a supremely good cook at home, why would I ever want to go out to dinner? So I'm afraid I've gone on writing when I actually thought I'd stopped!

This book began a long time ago although I was unaware of it at the time – perhaps as far back as my student days when I found myself fascinated by the study of other religions (my own being Christianity).

India was a stimulus. It is over fifty years since I was sent there by a church living in the past which believed that more missionaries were desperately needed by a church which hadn't a clue what to do with us when we arrived. I was hopelessly out of place and unsuitable. But after my three years in India people felt I ought to have added to my knowledge of Hinduism and Islam, if of nothing else. And so, from time to time, I was invited to lecture – something which continued after I left the church.

So, more formally, parts of this book began in Surrey as a series of WEA lectures which I thoroughly enjoyed. And parts of it began with a series of lectures at the South Place Ethical Society at Conway Hall in Red Lion Square in London. On both occasions I felt very privileged to be allowed to give these lectures.

Recently I have felt that I wanted to revisit them, to re-examine the subjects they cover, and to tidy up yet another area of my studies as my own ration of time begins to run out.

1

Passengers on a Bus

We are all of us travellers on a bus. Everything we need for the journey is to be found on the bus. But it is all a bit spartan and bare and comfortless. The journey began very slowly but the bus seems to be travelling faster and faster, almost careering out of control, and none of us knows its destination. That is not surprising because there is no driver. So the only thing we know is that we are headed for disaster and there is no way out.

The practical ones among us, those who are skilled with their hands, the technicians, the scientists, all set about making life on the bus better, easier and more comfortable. Every material good has come from them and all the games with which we fill our time.

Unfortunately, some of those games have led us to come to blows because they have made us competitive and given us an overwhelming determination to win. And so practical people have devised ever more devastating ways of coming to blows. Tragically, the very people who have done so much to make life on the bus better are the same

14

people who have made it almost unbearable. Every material good and every material evil has come from them.

Meanwhile there are some of us who have no practical skills at all. We are the people brilliantly described by the old toilet graffito: 'Sometimes I sits and thinks and sometimes I just sits.'

Some of us are just sitting on the bus, thumb in mouth, looking out of the window blankly and seeing nothing as it hurtles on its way. But some of us are sitting thinking. As he grew older my Dad used to say that he loved to spend his time speculating. As a family we were universally rude about his speculations because they seemed to go round and round in circles never actually getting anywhere. Perhaps you remember the old song: 'Running around in circles; running around in circles; running around in circles getting nowhere.'

That is a perfect picture of the people I am now beginning to try to describe: the men and women of religion and the men and women of irreligion too; the philosophers, the ethical thinkers and the theologians. Through thousands of years they have asked the same questions and all of them have come up with different variations of the same answers. They have created powerful organisations giving useless people power over the weak and the helpless. They have built huge and dominating buildings; created dogmas and creeds; done their best to satisfy their own greeds; lived out their lives intolerant of others and persecuting those who fall within their power but in spite of it all, through thousands of years they have made virtually no progress in their thinking.

If that sounds far too negative and critical, as I'm sure it does, just think for a moment about the major religions and philosophies. All of them look back to ancient teachers and their teachings and all of them just rehash the old teachings because they have nothing new to say. All of them really are just 'running around in circles'.

Francis Bacon was scathing about them. I have modernised his English, but very roughly what he said was, 'Many of the scholastics were men of great wit, far above my own, yet they have produced nothing. All the learning that hath been these many hundred years hath not brought about a single invention or brought to light one effect of nature before unknown.'

If Francis Bacon was right; if philosophers, theologians and ethical thinkers really are just 'running around in circles getting nowhere'; is there any point in looking at them at all?

I hope to be able to show that there is. If there isn't, then the whole of my own thinking has been a complete waste of time! A very large number of people are in the same boat.

In very general terms I DO think that all the basic thinking has been done and that, in these subjects, we shall come up with nothing new. We shall simply find that every seemingly new thinker is only really restating things that have been said before.

This is quite different from the scientist and the technician who are both moving into new territory all the time.

For me, the value in studying the thinking of philosophers, theologians and ethical thinkers lies in sifting for gold. All the thinking may have been done but it doesn't all have the same value. Indeed, a great deal of it has no real value at all. So we need to sift through it, like the old prospectors. In my books on the Bible and the Gospels that is precisely what I have tried to do, in the belief that there were good things to be found – good things and useful things.

In this book I want to cast my net wider. I want to look at some of the things people have tried out, some of the things people have thought as they have tried to make sense of life and to cope with all that it has thrown at them. Although my gaze will wander all over the world, if I am to keep this book within fairly restricted bounds, I shall have to be very selective and some parts of the world will barely get a mention.

I claimed that these thinkers are all running around in circles. Sometimes those circles solidify and become systems or rings of thought. Think for a moment of a bangle or a necklace made of intersecting rings.

To the casual eye each ring is identical so the bangle can be worn any old how and it will always look exactly the same. Of course, a scientist with a microscope will be able to point out that there are minor differences between the rings, and perhaps we shall discover some of those differences as we travel through this book.

But it is because the rings are so similar that it doesn't matter very much whether they were made at the beginning of the bus journey or many thousands of years later. They are still pretty much the same. So is there anything of value in their thinking at all? There OUGHT to be, because circular thinking is sometimes concerned with where people were before they got on the bus; and it is sometimes concerned with where people will go after they get off the bus; but most of all, it is concerned with persuading people to sit in their own seats and showing them how to get on with people sitting in other seats. In other words, it is concerned with how we should behave while we are on the bus.

Sadly, there is another respect in which that image of circular thinking solidifying into rings is apt. The bangle surrounds the wrist. The necklace surrounds the neck. The thinkers I have listed above often seem to want to surround us with a barbed wire fence or to fix us in our bus seats with seat-belts which cannot be released. They want to imprison us within their own system, and I find myself going back to another old popular song which Bing Crosby used to sing and which I loved as a youngster: 'Don't fence me in. Give me land, lots of land and the open skies above. Don't fence me in.'

But I have no wish to end this introductory chapter on a negative note. If there is any value in philosophical, theological or ethical thinking, it is of value through every stage and transformation of human existence, and it will continue to be of value until we finally become extinct.

If circular thinking has any value it will be both universal and timeless. It will be universal in the sense that any thinking man or woman anywhere on the bus; any thinking person of any generation, anywhere in the world, can come upon it. And it will be timeless in the sense that its value is not changed by any of the changes that have otherwise dominated our human lives over the centuries. It has the same value 'yesterday, today and forever'.

2

Our Earliest Forefathers

Our earliest forefathers found that they were in for a very bumpy ride indeed, although probably not a particularly long one. Food was often difficult to come by, hard to find and it often needed to be killed. With little shelter, the weather could be devastating and sometimes natural disasters overwhelmed them.

Any farmer can tell you how uncertain life is when you are dealing with the world of nature. Winds, droughts, floods; rain when you want sunshine and sunshine when you want rain; diseases, accidents; soils that are too heavy or too light; nothing in nature is ever quite straightforward. And to all of that our forefathers would have added such things as the darkness of the wildwood with its wild animals, venomous snakes, and all sorts of other imagined wild and dangerous creatures, ghosts and spirits. And as if all that were not enough, from time to time they had trouble with their neighbours.

The linear thinkers among them began to make tools, weapons, traps for prey. They began to learn how to herd and domesticate cattle, sheep and goats, how to make friends with wolves. They learned to harness fire, to grow crops and to distinguish between plants that were useful either as food or medicine and plants that were harmful. They learned to make clothes and to build houses that would give them some protection from the weather.

And while they were quietly going about their business the circular thinkers were wringing their hands and worrying. How on earth were they to survive? They worried about health, fertility and the continuance of their group. They were concerned to establish or restore some kind of harmony between themselves and the natural world. And they wondered about the natural world. Was it just what it seemed or was it imbued with a life of its own, with spirits, powers, elements that needed placating, pleasing?

They imagined a host of spirits and gods inhabiting trees, stones, streams, rivers, hills, mountains, the sea, the sky, the sun, the moon and the stars. How on earth could they keep on the right side of all these spirits? How could they avoid making them angry? How could they please them? And if they got things wrong, if they angered the gods, how were they to put things right, how could they placate them?

So, as if life were not hard enough already, they filled it and surrounded it with unnecessary fears and shadows and spent a great deal of time, energy and effort (and in the course of time, wealth) on a host of things that didn't exist except as figments of their vivid imaginations.

All over the world they populated the world and its space with legions of imaginary spirits and all over the world they tried similar ways of dealing with them.

In some areas of the world those similarities are not surprising. Hunter gatherer families grew into tribes and tribes grew to the point where their territory could not sustain them so there began to be widespread migration, and as people spread far and wide their ideas spread with them, and their language too. So, for example, in both north and south Europe and across into India, we find the languages which grew from the early Indo-Aryans and we find their gods too.

And across east Europe far into Chinese Asia and even across the other way to North America, the horse riding nomads and the Mongol empire spread their own ideas. It is remarkable how widely ideas can spread and how swiftly. Much later in human history Buddhist ideas began to spread because the Buddhists were excluded from their own country. Islam spread widely through conquest. The slave trade and then indentured labour meant that huge populations of people were transported far from home, all of them with their own cultures and history and ideas which they took with them. And in recent centuries, European empires have carried Christianity all over the world.

But even without all of that, people did come up with similar ways of coping with the spirit world. They used alcohol and drugs;. music and dance; astrology and various kinds of magic. And they used repetitive recitation; ritual and prayers; sacrifice of crops and birds and animals and even of people.

And alongside all of this, people used their artistic and creative skills to make representations of their gods or to bring colour to the rocks and stones where spirits were to be found.

But again and again I find myself sounding a note of caution as we look this far back. Cave paintings are often used as evidence of religion. Could they not just as well be evidence simply of the beginnings of a lasting human delight in art, and especially the thrill an artist has?

Similarly, hosts of small images have been found. There are figurines from Romania dating right back to 5,000 BCE which depict a mother with her child, later a favourite motif particularly in Egyptian and Christian religion. And there is a great deal of primitive painting emphasising the mothering breasts of female gods; just as there are hosts of figures and fertility images with erect penises.

It is not surprising that societies long dominated by religion claim a religious connection with all of these things and most of the time they are probably right.

But were NONE of these figurines simply mothers and children; none of the images simply dolls for children; none of those figures with erect penises simply forerunners of the naughty gargoyles littering our cathedrals?

We are sometimes told that ancient burial sites give us our first inklings of ancient religion. Some burial sites are quite clearly associated with the sun and the moon, which leads people to assume that the sun and the moon were worshipped. There is certainly other evidence for the importance of the sun and the moon in early thinking – but I can't help thinking of Brunel's railway tunnel near Bristol which was designed to let the sun shine right through on Brunel's birthday! And I think too of what was always called the ancient temple of Serapis which is now known to have been no more than a covered market. I have read of similar examples. We often impute religion where there was little or none.

I'm sure that burial sites often do demonstrate that there was a religious dimension to people's thought, but there are times when I wonder whether three other elements of human thought were not even more important. There is the desire to pay proper respect to those who have died (evident in Beowulf). There is the desire for a last resting place which mourners can visit. And there is also the desire to show off, to demonstrate power and human significance or importance. These things are human, not religious.

Religious people can often claim too much. We can easily read too much into the past but we must also be careful not to read too little.

As people tried to please or placate the gods and spirits their fertile imaginations had created, religions and religious philosophies began to develop and become more thoughtful and sensible. And ethical systems began to develop too.

Sometimes ethical systems developed as a response to the assumed wishes and dictates of the gods. When that happened people assumed that religion and ethics belonged together and religious people assumed (and still assume) that you can't have one without the other.

But, of course, that is nonsense. As we shall see, Confucius, the Buddha, the ancient Greeks, all developed very careful and thorough-going ethical systems without any reference to the gods at all.

So religion and ethics often grew together, but not always. There is no necessary connection between the two. Sometimes ethics developed as people tried to find the best ways of living in harmony with one another, and as a means whereby the weak could protect themselves against the strong, or as an attempt by the old to curb the passions of the young.

The methods people used to deal with the parallel universe of the spirits and gods have continued to be used to this day. Some of the great religions would disown many of them and I plan to go on to examine some of those. But in the early days of our history they were all serious attempts to create a spiritual system which can sustain us throughout our lives and in or beyond death. They were all about our relationship with the spirit world, with nature and with one another.

The world of the spirit seems to have been thought to have even greater reality than the world of the senses. Spirit was ultimate meaning and reality. And it is curious how often human thinking developed in similar ways and with similar patterns, the precursors of a great deal of later religious and philosophical thought.

Virgin births were common – often as a means of uniting the spirit world with the human; gods with us. The motif of the mother and child was always powerful.

Numbers were always important and some of them seemed to acquire a sacredness of their own. So, as people began to focus their worship on just a few gods of growing importance, they often ended up with triads of gods. And finally people often seemed to end up with one single over-arching and often remote spirit or god; a spirit or a god who could dissolve into a philosophical idea: the creative Mind; the All.

There is one of the great religions which embraces just about everything I have been writing about. Beneath its umbrella you can still find all the thoughts, ideas and methods of primal religion. But you can also find highly developed, sophisticated forms of religion that will cater for almost anyone, and these lead on to some of the most refined philosophical thinking the world has known, even including atheistic thinking. But in addition to that, this religion has spawned two of the great atheistic systems: Jainism and Buddhism of which more later. Hinduism is, of course, the religion to which I refer and which I wish to examine in greater detail later.

b

3

'The Same Yesterday, Today and Forever'

I read once that there were human beings in the British Isles for 50,000 years (or was it 30,000) before there is any evidence of religious belief.

The fact that there is no evidence does not necessarily mean that there was no religion but it may do. My own guess is that the earliest human beings had quite enough to do, just managing to get by and scrape a living, without bothering themselves about anything else. To speak of belief or unbelief is meaningless. They just hadn't got that far.

But when people first began to consider the possibility that the world was not just governed by nature, natural events, the weather, the availability of food and so on; then some people began to think of the possibility that there were powers, spirits and gods, and that we had better pay attention to them and try to keep them happy. And so religion was born.

My own conviction is that ALL religion is a human

construct and that unbelief, irreligion, call it what you will, has always lived alongside religion. If I am right, the earliest human beings had no religious ideas or beliefs at all. But it wasn't long before religion began to be a part of human life.

Primitive religion spawned a host of practices. Most of them are still in circulation although many of them are no longer associated with any of the major religions.

I'm not aware that anyone still studies the entrails of animals and birds before deciding whether to go into battle or not, although I wouldn't have put it beyond one or two political leaders I could mention. Nor do I know whether people still consult the oracle at Delphi. Why would they when every newspaper has its Agony Aunt?

Voodoo, sorcery, fetishes, charms, spells, curses, witchcraft, anything with magic power; the occult, astrology, images, relics, dietary laws – all of these things featured in primitive religion. And anything that seemed mysterious, hidden or unknown, soon suggested the need for some kind of sacerdotal priesthood set aside and armed with powers and authority to do for us the things we cannot do for ourselves. So mystery also featured very powerfully in primitive religion.

All of these things are to be found, to a greater or lesser degree, in modern society and many of them are to be found in the great world religions. Although it has to be said that religions have also dissociated themselves from many of these things – sometimes, as with witchcraft, very forcibly and with great cruelty. Let me skim through some of the things on my list just as they pour through my mind:

Diet is a never-ending concern of the media so it is obviously important to a host of people. But it is also important to some religions. Hinduism, Judaism and Islam all have forbidden foods – probably originally on health grounds.

Astrology is something else important enough to many people to merit daily newspaper space. Hinduism loves it but the great monotheisms frown on it, sometimes fairly fiercely.

Images play an important part in the life of Hinduism, Mahayana Buddhism and Catholic Christianity. And in Catholic Christianity there is still a great deal of affection and reverence for relics even though many of these have been shown to be fraudulent. I once read an estimate that there were enough pieces of the true cross of Jesus to make three crosses.

Sacerdotal priesthood is still an essential element in the Roman, Orthodox and Anglican sections of the Christian Church. Priests claim divine authority over their fellow humans and supernatural power: the power to do things ordinary mortals cannot do, such as celebrating the Mass and pronouncing absolution from sin. Priests love to surround their work with an aura of mystery even though there is no real mystery about what they do. That is one of the reasons ridiculous and unscientific ideas about what happens to the bread and the wine in the Mass continue to be held.

Outside religion, the occult and the paranormal continue to have a fascination for plenty of people.

I mentioned witchcraft earlier. Although it was condemned so roundly and persecuted with such cruelty and bigotry, it survives and even flourishes; although it has often morphed into the teaching and practice of complementary medicine (which, I hasten to add, is not intended as a veiled criticism of either witchcraft or complementary medicine. It is just that some of the genuine old witches often had a rudimentary, traditional knowledge of the helpful and harmful properties of plants).

However important any of these things may seem to be, especially to those to whom any of them matter, the only point I wish to make about them is that, like everything else in religious and philosophical thinking, these things belong to the realm of circular thinking. They mean pretty much the same now as they did thousands of years ago.

In the main, they are not things that interest me. I have little time or sympathy for them. As a result I am happy to move on fairly quickly to some of the more fundamental elements of religious worship and life. Or perhaps not quite so quickly after all.

4

Priesthood

Humans had not been around all that long before some people began to hunger for power over their neighbours. Parents had power over their children. Expert hunters or extra-strong warriors found that other people deferred to them – and they liked it! And some bright people who were too physically weak to impress their peers began to realise that they could exercise a different kind of power. If they could convince others that they had special knowledge and special gifts; knowledge relating to the unknown world of spirits and gifts enabling them to deal with those spirits; then even expert hunters and extra-strong warriors might defer to them.

So began the long, long story of medicine men, witch doctors, astrologers able to read the stars, soothsayers, people able to communicate with the dead, witches, quacks and priests.

They used magic, myth and mystery. They found that they could excite people's emotions with song, dance and repetitive ritual, and they were not above using alcohol and drugs to induce states which were thought to be beyond normal life and therefore some kind of entrance into a life of the spirit.

They also soon learned to persuade people to give gifts – technically gifts to the spirits and gods. Gifts from their produce and the very best of their livestock, all of it offered to the gods and eaten by the priests who no longer had to work for their living.

Gifts were given to persuade the gods to be kind, reliable, generous. The gods had to be persuaded to make people, cattle, sheep, goats and fields fertile and to be kind with the weather.

And if they were, then extra gifts had to be given to say thank you.

But what if they were not? Were the priests to blame? Had they failed in their duties as mediators and intercessors? Of course not. It was the general public who were to blame, or perhaps unpopular scape-goats among the general public. They had sinned!

And so sin came into the vocabulary of the priests. If they could persuade people that they were bad then they could blame everything on that badness. And they could persuade people that they needed the priests to find ways to make them good, priests who could find out how they could be forgiven, how they could be set on the right path; how they could find or achieve salvation.

And of course, one of the ways was to bring yet more gifts – indeed to be so generous in giving that you could be said to be making sacrifices. And what is the greatest sacrifice that anyone can make? Human sacrifice.

But even the priests didn't ask people to sacrifice themselves! A son would do, although even that was perhaps asking too much. How about a daughter? A daughter was surely expendable?

Faced with such demands, people came up with rather better ideas of their own. Prisoners of war were useful as slaves but they were expendable and if you ran out of them you could always have a battle and replace them, and if you could collar their wives and children, that was even better. Any of them could be sacrificed. In South America, masses of them were sacrificed.

Priests became very powerful indeed, often on a par with military and political leaders, nor have they entirely lost their power even now. Although in my lifetime, in countries like England, ordinary people have lost their fear of them, politicians still defer to them and buttress their lives with the support of taxpayers' money.

Let's look again at some of the methods priests have used.

5

Worship and a Way of Life

Nowadays television familiarises us with all sorts of religious festivals: Hindus bathing in the Ganges; Moslems on pilgrimage to Mecca; Catholic Christians flocking to hear the pope and others celebrating Easter or Christmas; or even occasions which some take dreadfully seriously when old local paganisms are recreated with dubious authenticity.

If you believe in a god or in gods you will feel that it is important to keep in touch with them; to know their will and to do it; to please them and to reap the rewards of doing so. People attempt to achieve these ends in a variety of ways which can all be summed up as their worship and their specific way of life.

Onc simple way of defining worship is through the memnonic ACTS.

A stands for Adoration, the first requirement of worship. This is not because the gods need us to tell them how wonderful they are but because we need to express our awe and wonder.

Or so I used to claim until I listened to the things that ordinary people were saying. Again and again they said that they couldn't believe in God because they didn't find him adorable or even admirable. Again and again, out of their pain or anger or both, they said, 'How can there be a God when s/he allows such dreadful things to happen?' Wars, violence, terrorism, personal tragedy, they all get thrown into the mix. People feel that God is all the time letting us down.

Although I know the arguments on both sides, it does seem to me that if people are to be persuaded to adore gods, they have first to be convinced that the gods are worthy of adoration.

The second element of worship: C, stands for Confession.

The gods of the higher religions are thought of as perfect. Indeed Aristotle went so far as to say that they are so perfect that they are incapable of doing anything else but contemplating their own perfection: navel gazing!

Yet they are quite unfair! Perfect themselves, they are said to have created us but to have created us imperfect – and yet they still expect perfection from us! When I said that once in a sermon, a neighbour of mine said, 'You ask and expect too much of us.' Not me. God or the gods.

They ask so much that whenever people worship one of the first things they have to do is to say 'sorry'. There are apologies and there is confession from 'miserable sinners' in desperate need of the 'bountiful mercy' of their gods.

As if we don't often feel bad enough about ourselves, a good deal of worship (certainly of Christian worship) has to do with impressing upon worshippers how evil they are. Quite ordinary, decent, upstanding people are expected to think of themselves as 'miserable sinners' in desperate need of the 'bountiful mercy' of their God and of the sacrifice of Jesus on the cross. As one Salvation Army friend of mine put it to me, 'Why do they always make us feel so bad about ourselves?'

I remember listening to 'conversion experiences' in which people spoke of the way Jesus turned their lives around from wickedness to the Christian way, but almost always their 'wickedness' was too trivial for anyone to pay any attention to it.

However, there *are* times when many of us slip up badly, and for religious people those are times for confession and for two more Cs: Contrition and Consecration.

Consecration to the life to which a god calls is certainly an important element in worship.

The third letter of our mnemonic is T and stands for Thanksgiving, a very considerable element in most serious worship. But once again, I have found that many people seem to feel that we have often got our priorities wrong. We spend so much time thanking the gods that we fail to recognise that it is people who really deserve our gratitude! When I was young 'grace' before and sometimes after meals was still common. As a young teacher, one of my elder brothers found himself in digs. He was not surprised when his first meal began with 'grace' but he was more than surprised when the man of the house said, 'Thank you to the cook.'

But why not? And why not 'thank you' to the shopkeepers, the farmers and the market-gardeners? And now that our food comes from all over the world, why not 'thank you' to a whole host of other people as well? Without all of them, the gifts of the gods would look pretty sparse and uninteresting. The Methodist annual covenant service used to contain the phrase: 'we have taken great benefits with little thanks'. It is a phrase which has haunted me all my life. But the question is, where should our thanks be directed?

For religious people the answer is simple: BOTH to their gods and to anyone else deserving of thanks.

The final letter of the mnemonic was S for Sacrifice. Very early in our history, priests learned to cash in on our fear of the gods and on the sense of sin they had created.

Once we were suitably contrite they associated the road back to acceptance by the gods with gifts and sacrifices.

Gifts keep the priesthood, if not in luxury, at least in comfort, free from financial worries and secure from hunger. And gifts provide buildings, buildings which glorify the gods through their magnificence and beauty (while worshippers get by in their hovels). These buildings also dominate the landscape and express the power of the gods. They can be objects of wonder but they can also oppress and become burdensome.

But how do we know whether our gifts have been adequate? It is a question asked right at the beginning of the Bible in the Cain and Abel story. Priests were very good at assuring us that a gift was not a real gift unless it was also a sacrifice. The gods were not content with our spares, whether our spare goods or our spare cash. They wanted the 'first-fruits'. Before we can enjoy the fruits of our labours we must FIRST bring our goods and gifts to the gods. For some this literally meant the first of everything including the first of our children. And since many of these sacrifices had to be burned as offerings to the gods, such demands were pretty awful.

And that led people to look for alternatives which would still manage to satisfy the insatiable appetite of their gods.

In Judaism, in spite of the prophets telling them that God desired 'mercy and not sacrifice', they went on sacrificing birds and animals until the destruction of the second temple after the death of Jesus. And in spite of the story of Abraham and Isaac there is evidence of occasional human sacrifice well into Old Testament times. But South America was the place where human sacrifice was the norm. In one study I read that one of their 'civilisations' sacrificed 30,000 people a year. I hope the study was wrong.

In Christianity the IDEA of sacrifice is still central to Christian faith. The New Testament suggests that Jesus saw himself as a once-for-all, final, perfect sacrifice, a sacrifice to end all sacrifices. His was the sacrifice which finally satisfied the hunger of God for the sacrifices of men because it met all of God's requirements.

And in some way which theologians have never really been able fully or satisfactorily to explain, Christians claim that the self-sacrifice of Jesus on the cross saves all the rest of us from our sins and enables us to enter into a father-child relationship with God.

Christian worship has at its heart a very simple re-enactment of the supper which prefaced the sacrifice of Jesus. No matter how complex and gorgeous the ritual which now often surrounds that re-enactment, the core of it is still very simple. Through the recital of the words of Jesus this is intended to be both a remembering of the past and also a present communion with God and with fellow worshippers.

Some Christians go much further than this. For them the bread and the wine actually, miraculously, become the body and blood of Christ. I don't want to be diverted by such primitive ideas or by some of the extreme behaviour these ideas lead to. The essential meaning of the rite is what matters and its value and importance for many, many people. A value which can spill out into ordinary, everyday life, giving extra significance to ordinary meal-times and dinner-parties.

But underlying all of this is the idea of vicarious sacrifice – the idea that one man's death can somehow wipe out my sin, make me pure, and reconcile me to God and God to me. That is an idea which seems to me to be a denial of personal responsibility which in turn reduces our worth and standing as human beings. Arrogant though it may sound, I believe that we must stand on our own feet, take responsibility for our own actions, and when we really go wrong, work out our own punishment and rehabilitation. I do not believe that anyone can do this for us. We stand or fall by our own dignity and worth as human beings.

I have spent my lifetime working with people. We are almost all fairly decent, kind, friendly, helpful and loving. Certainly we all have our faults and weaknesses and if we are pushed to the limit we can do some pretty desperate things. And yes, there are a few who do pretty awful things without being pushed to the limit.

But to suggest that most of the people I have met over a long lifetime actually need the sacrifice of a human being on a cross before they can become acceptable to God is to paint a pretty awful picture of God.

Of course, religions don't focus on sacrifice all the time.

Many are content to ask us to be generous, to live our lives decently and to adhere to a particular set of ritual requirements. The Moslem with his daily discipline of prayer times is an obvious model. Ritual requirements are not sufficient of themselves of course. They are intended to underpin a particular way of life. They call worshippers to dedication to God and to the way of life the gods have taught us to follow.

In all the major religions, the way of life worshippers are called to follow is a pathway of real purity and quality and it is this, more than anything else, which can make religion wonderfully attractive. When people manage to combine high ethical standards with modesty, gentleness, warmth and love, they become very attractive human beings indeed.

But whether we actually need religion in order to live such lives of high ethical standards and warm humanity is another question which we must pursue in due course.

Before I move on, I want to add a paragraph or two about prayer.

Prayer is the expression of the individual worshipper's relationship and communion with the gods. It is intended to be a two-way process. On the one hand there is the worshipper speaking to, thinking about, communing with the gods. And on the other hand the gods remind the worshipper of what they require, and assure the worshipper of divine love and support.

Prayer is time out from a busy day and is intended to be the fundamental focus and basis of a worshipper's life, setting everything else in life within the context of our relationship with the gods and underpinning our determination to live our lives according to the way the gods have set before us.

When I look at religion it seems to me that this emphasis on spending time quietly every day – time out from the demands of the day – is one of three immensely valuable things that religion has to offer. The others are a sense of community and the concept of a specific way of life to be followed. These are not things that are peculiar to religion but they are things which are common within religions, and they are all three thoroughly important elements in human life.

6

'All Things to All Men' and All Women Too!

And so at last, after all my diversions, we reach Hinduism. When I was a boy studying a Dickens novel for school certificate and then for higher school certificate, I came to the conclusion that all I needed to do was to skim through the book and then study the last chapter carefully. I didn't need to study the whole book!

The same is more or less true if you are studying the history of human religious and philosophical thought. If you are feeling lazy and don't want to work too hard or study too hard, there is a way out. All you need to do is to study Hinduism and then add a few minor tweaks here and there. Virtually the whole story is there.

Although present day Hinduism does seem to have avoided most of the worst excesses of the primitive religions of Africa and some parts of the far east (Borneo comes to mind). There, things like voodoo, sorcery, fetishes, charms, spells, curses and witchcraft are still common but, on the whole, Hinduism seems to have avoided many of these things.

Unlike some of the other religions that have a very specific focus, Hinduism is like an octopus. It can change shape and colour to be whatever you want it to be. It can and does embrace literally everything circular thinkers have ever thought or felt. It really can be 'all things to all men' and to all women too. As Pandit Nehru put it in his book *The Discovery of India*:

Hinduism as a faith is vague, amorphous, many-sided, all things to all men. It is hardly possible to define it, or indeed to say precisely whether it is a religion or not, in the usual sense of the word.

In its present form, as well as in the past, it embraces many beliefs and practices, from the highest to the lowest, often opposed to or contradicting each other. Its essential spirit seems to be to live and let live.

Sadly, even within this most tolerant of religions, there are those who use Hinduism as a part of their own intolerant and exclusive, aggressive nationalism. But that is a misuse of their religion, even though Hinduism is closely intertwined with the land of 'Mother' India, its social system and its history.

What follows is in no sense an academic study of Hinduism. All that I want to do is to try to show something of its comprehensive nature – its portrayal of the way human beings have actually gone in the development of their religious and philosophical ideas; and the supreme and sublime heights to which human thinking can take us (if we wish to follow that particular path).

Let me take you on a cycle ride with or without some of my students. We set off on our bikes from Medak, a small town fifty to sixty miles north of the twin cities of Secunderabad/Hyderabad in South India.

We cycle along a single-track footpath that leads us into the forest (forest, not jungle). It is open and colourful, for many of the trees become vividly colourful during some seasons of the year. The path comes to a parting of the ways. Where the paths separate a few stones have been gathered together and someone has lit a small fire which is just ash now. There has been an act of worship to ensure the goodwill of the spirit of the path that is to be followed.

We cycle on and come to a small river. In the monsoon season it will be a raging torrent perhaps 50 yards across but it is placid now, not very deep and only a few yards wide. We get off our bikes and are about to wade through when we see more signs of worship. The spirit of the stream, who can become so very dangerous, needed to be placated before the crossing was made.

In the middle of the stream is a large boulder brought down in a previous monsoon. On the boulder are more signs of worship and on the further bank, more still.

We cycle on past a hill and a large outcrop of rock. Parts of the rock are painted in whites and reds. The whole of nature is full of vibrant life, so trees, rocks, waterfalls and streams all become shrines and the places where there is water become places for ritual ablutions and for purification.

Our destination is a small village. On the edge of it there may well be a small shrine dedicated to the favourite god of the village – its patron god if you like. In the houses are small images – for worship or just (like the figures and figurines in my English home) for decoration? A bit of both I suspect! Our destination is one of the poorest homes in the village. The people here can't afford figures and figurines. They can barely afford to live. In the small yard where they do most of their cooking there is a small, standing display of sticks and leaves. It is the closest they can come to creating their own image of the god/spirit of their home and hearth.

Sometime later I sit chatting with a Hindu brahmin, a member of the Hindu priestly caste. He's an interesting character. Deeply devout, every day you can hear him reciting considerable passages of the Hindu scriptures as he does his daily devotions.

Yet when his wife is ill, his own need for ritual purity means that he can't look after her or tend her. He can't even be in the same room with her. Other people must care for her. He can only pray for her.

I tell him about my journey to the village. Does it worry him that for so many people in India religion is so primitive?

'Why would it worry me? Our religion is one that meets the needs of all kinds of people. For simple, ignorant villagers, there are the spirits and gods of nature. They know that all that they have to do is to keep those spirits and gods happy and all will be well.'

I wanted to interrupt with all sorts of comments and questions but you don't interrupt a Brahmin in full flow.

'Of course,' he continued, 'educated people like us know that none of these gods and spirits really exist. As these people grow more educated they will learn that there are very few real gods and that these are far greater than their village gods and spirits. But they will not be distressed for they will come to understand that all their prayers and worship have been seen and understood by the great gods worshipped by educated, thinking Hindus.'

He told me how, over time, Hinduism had focussed on just a few gods, one or two coming to the fore and then slipping into the background as others supplanted them.

'Nowadays,' he said, 'we have three gods, a bit like you Christians' (it was useless to try to put him right). 'Our three are Brahma the creator. He is lord of all creatures and above and beyond our worship. Then there is Vishnu. He is the god who controls our human lives. And he has had a number of incarnations. If you Christians weren't so arrogant and dogmatic you would perhaps realise that your Jesus is one of his incarnations, perhaps to be identified with Krishna.'

I knew a bit about Krishna, one of the most popular of all the Hindu gods, perhaps because he was such a sexy, naughty, mischievous god. My picture of Jesus didn't fit this image at all. But my friend had moved on to the third of his trio, Shiva and to his wife Kali, otherwise known as Durga. I have always found it hard to understand the appeal of Shiva and Kali. Together they symbolise destruction, judgement and death and they can be very terrifying indeed. But perhaps it is partly because they are so terrifying that they are fascinating – like horror films. But since Shiva is also a god who recreates new life and since Kali is also known as the 'great mother', perhaps they are also worshipped for those positive aspects of their divinity.

Having talked about these three, my Brahmin friend said, 'So you see, our educated Hindus have just as sophisticated and highly developed a religion as you Christians have. Our Brahma is the equivalent of your Father; our Vishnu is even greater than your Jesus, who, as I have suggested, may even be one of Vishnu's incarnations; and our Shiva and his wife Kali equate to your Holy Spirit and the mother of God, Mary.'

I did manage to tell him that I didn't buy his equation but he still hadn't finished with me.

'Leslie,' he said, 'there is yet more to see and to understand. You see, we Brahmins have carried understanding still higher. For us, even those three gods are not enough, for we know that just like us, they have no independent reality. There is only one reality: Brahman is all.

'Through our disciplined religious exercises and yogic meditation; through renunciation and purification; and after many lives it is possible for us to reach the point where our individual selves can attain deliverance and emancipation from the cycle of rebirths. Without losing our individual selfhood we can be gathered back into Brahman, the one reality from which we came and to which we go.'

In that one conversation I had been given a picture of the whole sweep of religious history, development and thought, not just as it has been in India but in very general terms, as it has been almost everywhere in the world. There are parts of that story on which I shall wish to focus in the coming chapters and there is one significant omission which will demand our attention, but in outline the whole story is there.

I have satisfied my own purposes in this chapter, but those who are really interested in religion will do well to study Hinduism properly. It is fascinating in its own right and also in the other religions to which it has given birth.

7

Monotheism

When I was still a Christian I sometimes used to give a lecture on the development of religion over the ages, beginning with a host of spirits and gods; whittling them down as in that picture of Hinduism in the last chapter; and finally ending up with monotheism.

It is difficult to say which of the great monotheistic religions came first, Zoroastrianism or Judaism. Judaism spawned Christianity and the two of them shared in the birth of Islam. There have been other monotheistic religions since. Two of the best known today are probably the Mormons and the Jehovah's Witnesses but those four were the groundbreakers.

Do they offer us one God in four guises or do they offer us four quite different gods? Zoroastrianism is only just a monotheism since the world is the battlefield between Good and Evil and there is no clear winner until the end time when Ahura Mazda finally triumphs.

Judaism offers us a God so holy and so awe-inspiring that he cannot even be named. Whenever his consonants appear, JHWH or YHWH, some alternative must be found such as 'the Lord'. This God came to be seen in such narrow, exclusive, racist terms in Old Testament times, that he has remained the God of the Jews and of nobody else.

But out of Judaism came Christianity. Christianity claims to be an inclusive and universal religion. Yet it tied itself to such a rigid credal theological orthodoxy that it has never stopped the squabbling within its own ranks and time and again it has excluded its own people – often with great persecution and violence. Its official picture of God is summed up in the doctrine of the Holy Trinity, not Father, Son and the Virgin Mary as I heard one Catholic priest define it, but Father, Son and Holy Spirit, three Persons, one God.

Islam returned monotheism to a simpler depiction of one God, Allah. The Moslem sees Allah as distant, one and alone. He will have nothing to do with the concept of God as a loving father because love implies both giving and receiving, and there is nothing that we can give to Allah. All the giving comes from him but fortunately he is gracious and merciful. Spreading originally through force of arms, it also claims to be a universal religion. But, like Christianity, it is riven by deep divisions, notably between Shi'a and Sunni Moslems. As I write, these divisions run so deep that Moslems are killing Moslems and creating havoc in parts of the Moslem world. Yet, at times Islam has proved to be remarkably tolerant towards worshippers of other monotheisms. The Jews of Spain were infinitely better off under Moslem rule than under Christian rule. On the other hand, Moslems persecuted Zoroastrianism almost to extinction in Persia. And there has often been incredible mutual hostility between Judaism, Christianity and Islam, a hostility which has included persecution, forcible conversion and war, and which continues to this day.

So; are Ahura Mazda, YHWH, the Trinity and Allah just different depictions of the one God or are they really four quite different gods?

If the religions' claims to be monotheistic are true, then they are just four depictions of the one God – usually portrayed as masculine though he needn't be, and at best, thought of as beyond masculinity or femininity. 'God is Spirit and they that worship must worship in spirit and in truth.'

I do not want to dwell on the horrors for which the three Judaic religions have been responsible. They turn many people off religion altogether. Instead I want to look at monotheism as man's supreme religious pilgrimage.

This is the way I used to think of it. Whether it is remains open to debate. It is arguable that the philosophical ideas of religions like Hinduism, Buddhism and Taoism which go beyond monotheism carry us further than monotheism does. But it is also arguable that they carry us beyond religion itself.

However, in this chapter I wanted to focus on monotheism by looking at just one of the ancient monotheisms I have mentioned.

But which one should I choose? Judaism or Islam, the two religions which are monotheistic in the simplest possible way? Christianity, which has complicated its monotheism with its doctrine of the Trinity and which has fractured so severely that there are, in effect, a number of quite different Christian religions? It would be quite fun to follow David Lodge's example and paint a picture of

Roman Catholicism as a game of Snakes and Ladders (in his novel *How Far Can You Go?*). It is, after all, a fairly accurate picture of the way Catholics used to be brought up and the things they were expected to believe.

Or shall I choose Zoroastrianism simply because in some respects it is the kindest and most human of the four. It also happens to be the least well known.

In the end I've chosen to write about none of them. It is easy enough to study any of them elsewhere. All of them are concerned about our relationship with God. All of them are concerned about the way we should live our lives (and I want to spend time on that later). And all (except perhaps Judaism) are concerned with our future after death. Both Christians and Moslems have their (sometimes vivid) ideas of heaven and of everlasting hell.

Although modern British Christians tend to ignore the concept of hell on the assumption that no decent God could condemn anyone in such a way, the idea is writ large both in the teaching of Jesus and throughout the New Testament. The oldest of us can still remember plenty of hell-fire teachers and preachers in both the Catholic and Protestant wings of the Church.

When I said that Zoroastrianism was the kindest and most human of the four, it was partly this concept of hell that I had in mind. In Zoroastrianism divine judgement is extremely fair. Think of a balance with our good deeds on one side of the scales and our bad on the other. If our goodness outweighs our badness we go to heaven. If the reverse, we go to hell – but not forever. Hell is a place of correction and is not everlasting. It leads to purification and, in a final renovation of all creation, to life with Ahura Mazda in total perfection.

I am not proposing to go on to a detailed study of Judaism, Christianity and Islam (there are plenty of them about). But I do want to end this chapter with a simple question. If we feel either that we want to be able to believe in a God or gods; or if we feel that we must; what kind of a God or gods do we wish to believe in?

The highly moral God of the monotheisms or the God of Zoroastrianism who is both highly moral and ultimately utterly fair and generous? Do we wish to worship the awesome God of Judaism and Islam, a God properly removed from us or do we wish to worship a God who is properly defined as Love?

Christianity speaks of God as 'Love' and claims that in Jesus God entered into our humanity – 'became flesh and dwelt among us'. Although, even in the New Testament and yes, even in the teaching of Jesus, it fails to sustain this picture of a loving God and presents a judgemental God instead. However, the notion of God as Love, pure and perfect Love, is perhaps the most attractive concept of divinity that man has ever managed to find. Christians would claim that we didn't find it! It was given to us by God, revealed in the coming and the life and death of Jesus.

8

Not Peace but a Sword

Before moving on I want to spend a little while considering why religions are so intolerant of one another and why they don't get on.

This is a story of family relationships. Family relationships can be very wonderful but they can also descend into the most bitter and intractable of all human relationships. Sadly, that has been the story of all the religions that feature in this chapter.

And we begin with the Jews. One of the lasting legacies and tragedies of the Holocaust has been the fact that it is no longer possible to tell the truth about the story of the Jews without being denounced as an anti-Semite so let me begin with a tiny personal note.

When I lived and taught in India, I condemned the caste system. One of my brightest students condemned me for it. After all, wasn't the class system in England just as bad? Sadly, he saw me as an Englishman criticising his beloved India. He failed to see that I was speaking, not as an Englishman, but as a Christian. So in India I condemned the caste system and in England I condemned the class system just as roundly. For both systems are fundamentally wrong and divisive. Both are a denial of our dignity as human beings.

So, if I criticise Jews, Christians, Moslems in this chapter, it is not because I am anti-Semitic, anti-Christian, anti-Moslem. It is because I am trying to tell the truth – the sad and sorry truth of family relationships that turned sour.

And we begin right at the beginning with Abraham, honoured by all three religions, but a man who couldn't stand up to his wife. Abraham had two sons. The first, Ishmael, was the child of a servant. The second, Isaac, was an unexpected late arrival born to his wife.

In the story, God and Abraham's wife Sarah combined to send Ishmael away to become the father of the Arabs. Isaac was the chosen one, the founding father of the chosen nation, the Jews.

To be God's chosen nation and yet to have no political power must be desperately difficult – even more difficult when the top layers of society are carried off into exile as happened under the Assyrians and the Babylonians. But those who remained struggled on and mixed with their neighbours until some of the Babylonian exiles returned. Led by Ezra, who was a particularly prickly customer, all offers of help from friendly neighbours were rejected, all mixed-marriages were broken up and it was insisted that from that time on Jews keep their race separate and pure.

The genealogy at the beginning of Matthew's Gospel makes it clear that there is no such thing as a pure race. Matthew speaks of three foreign women who all played a significant part in the lineage of the Jews' ideal king: King David.

But in spite of the facts, and in spite of the message of the prophets that Judaism was for all nations, it was Ezra's policy which won through. The Jews were not to be leaven mingling with the peoples of the world and sharing the riches of their religion with the world. They were to be an exclusive, separate, chosen nation and ultimately Jerusalem was to dominate the world. Sadly, it often has dominated the world for all the wrong reasons.

Now throw Christianity into the mix. I'm no great lover of the apostle Paul but it is to his lasting credit that he was the one who saw that the message of Jesus was a message for all the world, not just for the Jews. That single inspiration was the making of Christianity but it rang the death-knell on any future success amongst the Jews. From that moment onwards the two brother or sister movements, worshippers of the same God, would go their separate and mutually hostile way. As long as neither of them had any political power that didn't matter very much.

But when the Christian Church obtained power in the later stages of the Roman Empire, trouble started. At first it was mostly one kind of Christian persecuting and slaughtering another. But then Christians began to persecute Jews. From the time of the Crusades onwards those persecutions were only partly about religion. They were often more about politics and scapegoating – very similar to today's demonising of 'immigrants', no matter who they are or where they come from. But at one time or another Jews were persecuted throughout Europe.

Meanwhile Islam had arrived. Muhammad learned from both Jews and Christians, and when he was in exile in Medina he made friendly overtures towards the Jews there and tried to interest them in his work. After all, they both looked back to Abraham, and Muhammad respected the work of the Hebrew prophets and was calling his own people to worship the one God.

His overtures were rebuffed in such a way that he retaliated by destroying the Jewish community with considerable violence. It was not a good start. Yet, in many places, as Islam spread throughout the middle east it showed considerable tolerance towards both Jews and Christians; and in Spain the Jews were far better off under Moslem rule than they ever were when the Christians finally drove the Moslems out.

Meanwhile there had been the Crusades. Focussed on Jerusalem these pitted Christians against Moslems. And when Christians proved to have only limited and temporary success, they turned against their fellow Christians and sacked Constantinople, preparing the way for its later incorporation into the Moslem world. Moslems have never forgotten or forgiven the Christians for the Crusades, something which became very apparent when George Bush spoke of his own crusade.

There has been mutual suspicion, fear and hostility between the two religions ever since the crusades. The worldwide spread of the two religions means that in all sorts of places they face one another or intermingle uncomfortably. As a result there is the danger of outbursts of religious hostility all over the world. This was seen fairly recently as Christian East Timor strove for independence from Moslem Indonesia. With Australia supporting East Timor, Osama bin Laden declared that the bombing in Bali, which claimed 200 lives, was Moslem revenge against the Australians.

Some flag-waving conservative evangelical Christians

in the USA will certainly see their fight against terrorism in terms of Christianity against Islam. And most of the terrorists of the present time (2013) seem to be Moslems. But neither set of people are doing anything which has anything to do with genuine religion. Their behaviour is condemned just as much as it is encouraged by both Christians and Moslems. Perhaps that has always been the case. I would like to think so.

The plain fact is that since the beginning of the 20th century it is power politics rather than religion which has been the real culprit. Perhaps that has always been the case. The First World War was certainly not caused by religion, but it saw Christians on both sides demonising Christians on the other and invoking the support for their side from the SAME God.

The latter end of the 20th century saw a number of curious situations where Christians were fighting in defence of Moslems against other Moslems or even against other Christians. Whatever the rights and wrongs of those fightings, few of them have been the result of religious differences, although sometimes religion has been a contributory factor.

But in conflicts where all the protagonists on one side are from one religion and all the protagonists on the other side are from another religion, then their religions exacerbate the situation power politics has created. Nowhere is that more clear than in the relationship between the modern state of Israel and its neighbours.

Hostility between Jews and Moslems has become far more intractable since the restoration of the Jewish state in Israel. This has its roots in religion and the exclusiveness of Judaism going right back to Ezra but, of course, it is far more complicated now than just the religious divide. Nevertheless, it has to be said that without religion there would have been no conflict in the first place and people could have lived in an intermingling harmony and peace from Old Testament times to the present day.

So often religion CLAIMS to offer a path to human peace but it proves to be one of the greatest obstacles to peace. Jesus was right when he said that he did not come 'to bring peace, but a sword'.

The family squabbles of Judaism, Christianity and Islam are well known. But in the west we know far less about the family squabbles in the Punjab. After the Moslem invasions there were two main religions in the Punjab, Islam and Hinduism. Sikhism took elements from both in a vain attempt to bring the two closer together and to create harmonious relations between them. In time, all that Sikhism did was to cause BOTH Islam and Hinduism to be hostile to this child born out of wedlock. Persecution and struggles for independence have been the continuing story on the frontiers of India and Pakistan. And the squabbles soon became part political, part religious.

But there is another reason why religions never manage to get on with one another. It is that so many religions claim to have or to be 'the truth' and there can only be one truth.

If one religion claims to be 'the truth' it follows that all other religions are, to put it at its kindest, in error. So the one religion believes that it must become universal and must monopolise the religious life of the world. Needless to say, that doesn't go down very well with any other religion claiming to be 'the Truth'. They all end up in competition with one another. And sadly, when any one of them achieves political dominance in a state, it tends to work very hard to extinguish all competitors.

Yet there is a great deal that is similar in many of them. As a result there have been attempts, as in the Bahai faith, to bring them all together. Sadly, such attempts are doomed to failure and will always only end up as the Bahais have done by adding one more to the sum total of the world's religions. All of which prompts me to want to look in two separate but related directions. I want to look beyond religion and I want to look at alternatives to religion.

9

Other Worlds Beyond Ordinary Human Experience.

One of the functions of religion is to carry us beyond the world we live in, the world of the senses, and to lift us into the world of the gods and spirits or just 'the world of the spirit'.

In groups or in crowds it seeks to achieve this through heightened emotion. It has not been above using alcohol or drugs but mostly it has used nothing more exotic than rhythmic music, song and dance and the emotional effect of being in a crowd where everybody is engaged in doing the same things at the same time.

Crowds have a life of their own and we can be swept away by the excitement and exhilaration of the moment.

I find myself thinking of King David of the Old Testament dancing before the ark (much to the disgust of his wife Michal); the disciples of Jesus on the day of Pentecost 'speaking in tongues'; early Christian congregations also getting carried away and speaking in tongues, something which led to some pretty firm words from the apostle Paul. I think of dancing dervishes whipping up their own emotions. And much nearer to our own time, I think of early Methodists in huge crowds swept away by the 'enthusiasm' of the moment and surrounded by the cold water of a pretty sterile, formal state Church of England. I think of the emotion deliberately roused by the great evangelists from Whitfield through Gypsy Smith on to people like Billy Graham and the modern American evangelists who all use crowd fever and song to whip up people's emotions. I think of modern Pentecostals, who continue to practice speaking with tongues and whose worship tries to free up the restrained and inhibited emotions of Europeans, and who are very successful in doing the same with less inhibited Africans and Americans.

And all this is designed to carry us beyond our normal, basic lives into 'the world of the spirit'.

Quite apart from religion there is a consistent desire on the part of many people, especially young people, to escape from the mundane, the boring, routine of daily lives. And again this is often achieved through crowds, whether the crowds at a football match or the crowds at a disco with its noise and flashing psychedelic lights and smoke and darkness.

Pop singers use the same experiences to whip up the crowds in their audiences. I remember attending such a concert where the singer himself was like a dancing dervish, with robotic supporting singers in the background and with flashing lights and coloured smoke. The whole experience made me feel that the man was just like a witch-doctor of old.

And with all this comes the use of alcohol and drugs, sometimes used to heighten people's experiences and sadly, all too often used to bring people to the point of oblivion.

Another, quite different attempt to experience other worlds also takes both religious and secular forms. There are those who are convinced that we are surrounded by the paranormal. Whether their interest, their investigations, their 'experiences' have to do with ghosts or spirits or UFOs, they are convinced that this ordinary world which we all know and experience and live in is not the whole story.

And in the religious world, there are those who, holding to this kind of belief, seek to achieve and maintain contact with the spirits of the recent dead. This is an area of life where there has been a great deal of hocus pocus and where most of us are sceptical. But to those who take this area of enquiry seriously, and to those bereaved who seek, and sometimes find, comfort, this is a very real world indeed.

Finally, there is another completely different and individual path into experiencing a world or worlds beyond our own. It is the solitary world of the hermit in his cave; the monk or nun separated from 'the world' and even from one another in a cell of their own choosing. It is a world of austerity and of self-denial.

By the denial of self and the punishment of the self, men and women seek to leave self behind and to enter into a mystical relationship, or even mystical union, with their god. Through their asceticisms, their disciplines and their complete aloneness, they escape into their own world of the spirit and into a level of experience which few of us can share.

61

Within Christianity I think of Jesus in the Garden of Gethsemane and of people like St. Francis of Assisi, Mother Theresa and St. John of the Cross. But these are only some of the best known. In the early days of Christianity the hermit seems to have been much more common than he is today.

I think of Christian mystics because that is the tradition in which I grew up, but there have been plenty of similar examples in other religions and it is only my own lack of interest in them and scepticism about mysticism generally which has led me to pay so little attention to them.

THEY believed that they were entering into some sort of faith-union with their god, a faith-union beyond the life of ordinary mortals. If sceptics like me explain all these experiences both of crowds and of individuals in terms of human psychology that doesn't alter the fact that they seem very real to those who enjoy or experience them. All too often they have no value except to those individuals who have them, but just occasionally they lead on to positive lives of real value and service to the wider community.

It is perhaps in Hinduism and Buddhism, with their concept of the All, that otherworldliness and spirituality reach their pinnacle. The goal of all human life is for us to return to the All from which we came. This is not achieved easily or lightly and it usually takes a number of lives before we can finally become ready for absorption back into the All.

So the concept is associated with some form of belief in reincarnation. Things like desire and ambition hold us firmly in their grip and it is only as we learn to let go and find release from all those things which bind us to earthly life and existence that we finally become ready to be absorbed back into the All. This is both our goal and our final destiny.

I called this the pinnacle of spirituality, yet it can also lead to a complete denial of spirituality. Those of us who see humans in terms of nature define us simply as one among the animals, a bundle of atoms brought together by the union of our parents. Death simply releases those atoms back into general use! The All is simply the sum total of everything that makes up this and every other universe.

10

Where Do We Come From?
Where Do We Go?

Am I right in thinking that it was in *The Ghost Train*, a film starring Will Hay, that the phrase kept cropping up, 'Where do he come from, where do ee go?' It was one of those things that grabs hold of teenaged boys, and for a week or two after seeing the film we kept on repeating it. It has stuck with me ever since.

Physicists like Brian Cox tell us that we come from 'energy'. Biologists like Richard Dawkins begin at the next bus stop and trace our story from its earliest beginnings until now. Some religious thinkers are happy to accept those findings but suggest that behind it all there is a great, universal, creative Mind God. Others prefer to bury their heads in the sand and to stick to ancient myths from ancient religions.

I find the scientific story far more fascinating and far more satisfying than the old myths. But that doesn't alter the fact that those old myths still have a great deal to teach us. They have their own fascination and their own message so they are worthy of our examination. That said, many of us are happy to accept that science can now tell us where we came from. But where do *we* come from, you and I?

At one level the answer is obvious. I came from the physical union of my parents and, as the fourth boy, I owe my existence to my father's desperation for a daughter! At that level it is also possible for most of us to trace our antecedents back a while.

But is that the whole story? Did we have any other pre-existence? It is claimed that Jesus did. Did we? Did we have previous lives as some people believe? Or are we the sum of atoms that have been used before, a gathering together of elements from all over the place? Or. . .

Since we have no memory of previous lives, speculation about them seems pointless. The questions I have been asking cannot be answered, and since they cannot be answered there is no point in bothering with them. Idle speculation is a waste of time and energy, and worry about such things is just plain stupid.

But what about the other end of life? After death is there anything more? Is death just the end or is there some continuing life? Now that IS something which bothers a lot of people, something which people have worried over for a very long time.

One of the reasons people have always turned to religion is that they cannot accept the idea that this life is all that we have. They want more. And in societies where life expectancy is still dreadfully short that is thoroughly understandable. A man of my age may well feel that he has done pretty well and may be quite content with the thought that death is the end. But when children or young adults die it seems all wrong that they should have had so little.

All through history there have been those who hankered after some sort of life after death. In ancient times those who longed for life after death had fairly vague ideas and a confused mixture of both hopes and fears. It was thought that the dead could still influence our lives (while there was flesh on the bones). So heavy stones were used to keep the dead down and to prevent them causing malicious harm to the living.

The idea that life goes on also sometimes involved ensuring that people went on their travels well equipped, so graves were filled with all sorts of possessions which might come in useful in another life: clothes, tools, weapons, jewellery, wives even, and horses and servants.

As people tried to develop their thinking, two kinds of idea became common: Hindus, Buddhists and others came up with some kind of reincarnation idea – the belief that we don't just live one life. We live a succession of lives usually with the goal of a progression towards absorption into the One, the All, the Ultimate Reality.

The other idea is more familiar to us in the West. It seems to have been developed first by a brotherhood of religious reformers in Palestine. They were known as the Hasidim and became the Pharisees of New Testament times.

It comes as something of a surprise to many people to learn that the Jews of Old Testament times had no real belief in life after death. Their ideas were not so very different from those of the Greeks. Hades or Sheol was the place of the dead. There, the ghosts or shades lived on in a fairly meaningless way.

The Hasidim developed the idea that after death there is a resurrection for those who have lived good or godly lives. A new life has been stored up for them with God. Christians took over this idea and developed it, supporting it with miracles such as the raising of Lazarus from death and the resurrection of Jesus himself. Moslems also took the idea over (initially from the Jews) and developed their own rather sensual idea of resurrection life. The hope of this life is one of the significant dreams set before the budding suicide bomber.

There are many variants of the resurrection idea and I don't propose to examine them here but I probably ought to mention that in addition to heaven for the saved, Christians also developed the idea of hell for the damned. Catholic Christians also had two further ideas. For people who have not been baptised into the Christian faith they provide a limbo which is very like the old ideas of Sheol or Hades. And for those who are fit neither for heaven nor hell they offer purgatory, a sort of afterlife place of preparation aimed at finally enabling people to enjoy the bliss of heaven.

The separation of people into those fit for heaven, those fit for hell, those for purgatory and so on involves ideas of judgement which litter the pages of the gospels. It needs to be stressed that although Christians are stuck with the New Testament, many of these ideas about life after death are in a constant process of change and challenge. I read recently that hell ceased to exist for Catholic Christians in the 1960s! There is a measure of truth in that tongue-in-cheek claim.

In addition to belief involving reincarnation or resurrection there are spiritualist claims that it is (sometimes) possible to make contact with the dead and to have limited converse with them. This is usually felt to be more likely in the days soon after a death. Although spiritualism has been attended by a great deal of hocus-pocus, there is no doubt that some hold these views with real sincerity.

All of these ideas depend on faith, hope, sometimes even just wishful thinking. There is often a strong desire when people die that we shall one day be reunited with them and see them again. Some religions offer these hopes as if they were certainties and there are many religious people who hold their beliefs with passionate conviction and certainty. That kind of certainty obviously brings comfort to them. But sadly, when people have that kind of certainty and try to impose their views on others, instead of providing comfort they often add to people's distress.

It is important to approach all these different ideas with sensitivity. Although some people on both sides of the religious fence are utterly sure that they are right, none of us can KNOW. Perhaps we would all do well to focus on the things that we do know, the things that can bring help, support and comfort to anyone who is bereaved, whether religious or not.

11

Religion and Ethics

Many years ago someone was explaining to me why he and his wife were choosing to send their children to the local Church of England school rather than to the local state school. It wasn't just because they felt it was a better school. It was because they felt that at the Church of England school their children would receive an education which included a good moral framework.

After all the revelations associating religious education with immorality in recent years I wonder whether they would still make the same decision. It seemed to me at the time that they were making the all too common assumption that you can't have ethics without religion.

The famous 'ten commandments' were inscribed on the walls of many an old church or chapel and my generation grew up with them. It is largely because of them that my generation also grew up assuming that there is a necessary link between religion and ethics and that you can't have one without the other. Any study of early Buddhism, of Confucius or of the ancient Greeks will show how very wrong that is. There is just as much concern with ethics outside religion as there is within it. Religious or not, decent people have always been concerned with trying to work out the best way in which we can live our lives. What is more, precisely because unbelievers are not tied to 'authoritative' divine commands in the past, they are perhaps best equipped to wrestle with ethical problems our forefathers never had to face.

However, in this chapter I simply want to look at some religious ethical teachings with which we are all familiar. Let us begin with those ten commandments. They are themselves an adaptation of an even more ancient code so, if antiquity is a recommendation, they have that to recommend them.

In Exodus chapter 20 the first seven verses are all about God and his command that we worship him alone. They have everything to do with religion and nothing to do with everyday life.

The same can be said of the command to keep a 'sabbath' day for worship, a day free from work. This command is justified by reference to the old creation account which claims that God created the world in six days. Few people would use that as a justification for any command today, but there is one sense in which both religious and irreligious people may feel that this 'command' has something to say to them. It points to the very simple fact that human beings do need a break from their everyday routine and toil and benefit when they have one.

It is the next group of commands that most people on the fringes of religion would regard as the ones that matter: honour your parents; do not kill; do not commit adultery; do not steal; do not bear false witness against your neighbour; and finally, do not covet the things other people have.

Those are principles which underpin virtually any ethical system anywhere in the world, ordinary basic principles for decent living. But notice how negative they all are, as if 'God' is speaking to little children.

I remember a psychologist saying that when our children are very little we spend all of our time like Joyce Grenfell in her famous sketch as a primary school teacher saying, 'Don't do that.'

As our children grow older that negative tends to be replaced with the positive 'Do this' or 'Do that.'

And then as they grow older still we replace dos and don'ts with the concept of being. This is the kind of person we want you to be or to become. It is a concept which is often left unspoken and which depends on example and on the example of ideal heroes: for Jews, Abraham, Moses David and the Prophets; for Christians, Jesus, and for some of them Mary and the saints; and so on. All religions and societies have their own.

There is, of course, far more to Jewish ethics than is mentioned in the ten commandments. Few, if any, religions have been so assiduous in the study of right behaviour in the face of the practicalities of everyday life.

Christianity owed a great deal to the Jews. When Jesus was asked to define the law of God many centuries after the ten commandments were first promulgated he quoted Jewish teachers who claimed that they could be summed up in just two very positive commands:

Love God with all your heart, mind, soul and strength and love your neighbour as yourself.

Again, there is far more to Christian ethics than this, even if this does sum up all the rest. In the New Testament itself, Christians will point to the parables of Jesus and to the Beatitudes. And in some of the New Testament letters we see some of the early Christians beginning to wrestle with the kinds of ethical problems they had to face in their own daily lives.

Examine any serious religion and you will find it looking at the way in which humans should behave and the way in which they should relate to one another and to the world around them. I'm not sufficiently familiar with Islam or with Zoroastrianism to expound or to expand on their ethical systems. But it may be of interest to mention the heavenly beings (like angels) created by Ahura Mazda for these demonstrate the kind of ideals and hopes all of us are encouraged to follow or strive after. They were named: Good Mind, Righteousness, Devotion, Dominion, Wholeness and Immortality.

When religions want to commend themselves to people who do not belong; when they want to persuade us to join their ranks; when they want to convert us; again and again they point to the quality of life to which believers are called and committed.

Sadly, one of the great stumbling blocks between religions and those of us who have no religion lies just here: in the complete failure of religious people to demonstrate any quality of life that is richer, purer or nobler than any other. This was first born in upon me when I lived in India in a society where Hindus, Moslems and Christians lived side by side and no one group stood out as in any way superior to the others. Now that Britain has become a multi-cultural society there is no need to go abroad to make that discovery.

However, it was back in this country, after I had left Christianity behind, that I first really began to acknowledge that unbelievers have their ethical systems too. And so, having spent so much time in this book looking at religion, the time has come for us to look at the many and varied forms of unbelief and at the ethical systems they have spawned.

d

12

Different Kinds of Unbelief

In an earlier chapter I mentioned a lecture I sometimes gave where I spoke of the logical progression from belief in many gods and spirits to monotheism, the belief in one single all-encompassing, all-knowing, all-seeing God: Ahura Mazda, YHWH, God the Holy Trinity, Allah or whatever name you choose to give to him or to her – strictly speaking neither him nor her but Spirit.

Sometimes when I gave that lecture I would wonder when I was going to be asked: if it is logical to move from belief in many gods to belief in one God, would it not also be a logical progression to move one step further to belief in no gods at all?

Nobody ever asked me the question!

I'm no longer convinced that logic has anything to do with it. Although it still seems to me that in some respects the monotheistic religions are superior to most of the old polytheisms 'it ain't necessarily so'. But what about unbelief? And is it really possible to speak as my chapter heading does of different kinds of unbelief? Surely unbelief is unbelief, and that's that?

Let's look at things rather more closely.

I read recently that the first evidence for human beings *in the British Isles* goes back 150,000 years. I don't know how far back the first evidence for religion takes us, but the first evidence of religion *in the British Isles* dates back less than 5,000 years. 150,000 years is a great deal further back than the figure I quoted earlier in this book.

That doesn't necessarily mean that there was no religion before 5,000 years ago in this country, but it DOES suggest that for a long, long time, early humans managed without religion perfectly well. It also suggests that, when it came, religion was something invented by humans.

What I am suggesting is that a lot of unbelief is the unbelief of people who for one reason or another, have never got round to thinking about gods or whether they exist. And it seems to me that that is still the commonest form of unbelief. I think it is also the commonest form of belief!

MOST human beings still lack the leisure which is required if we are to think about these things. They are still too wrapped up with just managing to survive to do more than follow where their parents and their parents, and so on before them, have led. If they are born into a religious society they do the religious things which seem to be necessary for survival but that is all there is to it. And in societies like our own, where religion is clearly not necessary for our survival, they don't bother their heads with it. This unthinking unbelief is by far the commonest form of unbelief that I come across in the course of my work.

It is similar to what I used to call rather rudely, 'Church

of England' unbelief! You can find it in any society where there is an established state religion. You will find it in Japan in the Shinto religion and you will find it in ancient Greece and Rome. In Confucianism you could almost call it a part of the Confucian Way! It tends to take one of a number of forms.

Most commonly people are agnostic. They don't know whether there are gods or no but if there are they feel that they are so remote and uninterested in us that there is no need to bother with them. Someone said of the world of Nature: 'Our indifference to nature is matched by nature's indifference to us.' This is the way these agnostics think about the gods. There is no need to waste time worrying about them, thinking about them, let alone paying them any attention.

But for the sake of public order they are quite prepared to go through the motions of the state ceremonial apparatus. In this country, until fairly recently, that meant that people were quite happy to call themselves 'Church of England' and to avail themselves of its services as rarely as possible. But even that is no longer as true as it used to be.

Before I move on to my next group, mention of the natural world has prompted another thought. The incredible and marvellous story of evolution has destroyed the old world view and led many people either to dismiss gods altogether, or to move them to such a peripheral role that they cease to have any real significance for us. But if that story of evolution did much to alter our concept of gods, the more modern awakening to the sheer, incomprehensible picture painted by astronomy seems to make it quite impossible to hold on to the old ideas of gods who are personally interested in and involved in us.

I read recently that there are 'about fifty million stars like the sun in our galaxy, and at least two hundred thousand galaxies in the Universe, each containing a roughly equivalent number of stars, or suns.'

And then I went out into the garden and disturbed an ants' nest. It seemed to me that belief in personal gods is like believing that I could be personally interested and involved with the life of each separate and individual ant.

But I have digressed. It is time to look beyond thoughtless unbelief and agnosticism to unbelief proper.

There are many of us who have no religious beliefs at all. We are not belligerent about it or evangelistic. Where we stand is important to us but we have no desire to make any attempt to impose our own world view on other people. But we do ask other people to respect the fact that we stand where we do quite deliberately and after giving the whole subject our careful attention.

We have looked at both belief and unbelief; we have examined the religion of our forefathers which is probably the religion of the society in which we live. And sometimes we have looked at religion more widely. We have come to the conclusion that the gods are the inventions of humans and that the whole cumbersome apparatus of religion could be dismantled without any significant loss. For us, religion's only value lies in the works of art and music it has inspired and in the sense of community it gives to many people.

We have no belief in the gods at all but we share with agnostics a willingness to go through the motions, to do whatever the state feels is necessary just for the sake of tolerance, peace and quiet. Indeed, we will often go even further than that in order to express our love, friendship and sense of solidarity with some of our friends or our nearest and dearest who hold on to their religious beliefs.

The last, and I think and hope, the smallest group of unbelievers is the group of fiercely belligerent atheists who will fight their corner whether there is a corner to fight or not. They are as prickly and difficult to live with as the most rabid of religious fundamentalists.

I had no sooner spoken of 'the last group' of unbelievers than I thought of another – you see how many there are! These are people who are anxious about the word 'atheist' and anxious about what they see as the narrowness or cold materialism of unbelief. There are still quite a lot of them about. They say to me, 'I am not religious but I like to think that I am spiritual.'

I am very careful never to press them too hard to define what they mean. Nor do I bother to attempt to put people right when they tell me that I am 'spiritual'.

At its best, this group of people reaches through religion to philosophical realms beyond religion and beyond what is knowable. You can find it in Hinduism and you could almost say that it defines both Taoism and Theravada Buddhism. And it has sprung up again recently in western Christianity in the teaching of people like Paul Tillich. Wherever there has been mysticism there has been a tendency towards this kind of 'beyond belief' ism. The mystics, the 'Sea of Faith' people, Taoists, Hindus and some Buddhists still cling to the language of religion and still think of themselves as religious people but they have gone beyond religion.

Where God is thought of as Spirit only or as the no-thing or the All we reach beyond the realm of words or the intellect into something amorphous and indefinable.

Cynics sometimes suggest that this is really a return to pantheism and to ancient beliefs that everything is infected with or inhabited by 'the All'.

Alternatively cynics may ask what is the real difference between 'the All' and nothing, and between being lost in the All and simply being lost.

Many people find this kind of beyond religion philosophical thinking and its mystical associations extremely attractive and think of it all as the very highest and noblest that religious thought and worship can achieve. It takes away all anthropomorphism from our concept of divinity. God IS Spirit.

But whether 'spirit' is anything or nothing is another matter altogether. People who are attracted by this kind of religion or irreligion consider that there is no division between the sacred and the secular. Life is one and all life is sacred. But of course, it is just as possible that life is one and all life is secular!

It is from *within other religions* that early Buddhism has been defined as atheistic, and it is that definition which enables me to include this kind of philosophical thinking as one of my forms of unbelief. I shall look at Buddhism more closely in a future chapter.

When you look at unbelief like this, it soon becomes clear that it is much more common than people in religion-based societies like to admit. Whole societies have been based on systems where there is no real religion at all. I've mentioned the very first generations of humans but in the far east neither Shinto nor Confucianism has ever been religious in any real sense of the word. In India, Jainism and original Buddhism – the Buddhism of the Buddha were both atheistic. (The later form of Buddhism, the

Buddhism of prayer wheels and images and so on, known as Mahayana Buddhism, took to itself all the paraphernalia of the ancient beliefs of the societies where it became dominant, but original Buddhism was free from all this.)

In the west, in ancient Greece and Rome, there was always considerable unbelief expressed in the teachings of people like Democritus, Epicurus and his disciple Lucretius, the Cynics and so on, and there was a great deal of the lip-service-to-the-gods kind of unbelief. And in modern times, Communism was atheistic.

Nor have we any means of knowing how many unbelievers there were or are in societies where it is dangerous to express your unbelief because religious authority is so dominant, dogmatic and destructive.

We know that there were unbelievers in that most theocratic of states, ancient Israel, if only because twice in the Psalms there is reference to 'the fool' who 'says in his heart, there is no god.' He probably didn't dare to say it out loud and the same may well be true in some Moslem societies today.

(It has nothing to do with my book but there was a time when I chose to use those psalmists to give me a title for a talk to humanist groups. When I quoted the psalmists and added, 'so we are all fools here' a lady in one of my audiences got up and walked out!)

If you want an accurate picture of the strength of unbelief, there is no point in looking at societies where religion is dominant and powerful. You have to look at societies which are relatively free and open. These make it very clear that unbelief of one kind or another is not just alive and well, but is extremely common. And one of the significant things that we shall discover as we look at unbelief rather more thoroughly, is that systems of unbelief all focus on ethics, which gives the lie completely to all those religions that denounce unbelief as not being ethically serious.

13

Unbelief in India

It was in India that the first known formal systems of unbelief were worked out. The earliest of them all was the Lokâyata or Cârvâka philosophy. It has a great deal in common with modern western secular humanism. Its origins are lost in the mists of time but it became the first full-blown naturalistic philosophy in history. Yet, even though it flourished from the sixth century BCE until the seventh century CE we would know very little about it if it were not for the writings of its opponents.

From their criticisms and arguments we learn that Cârvâka philosophers repudiated the old religion with all its superstition, ritual and magic. It rejected the gods. It rejected the Hindu sacred books, rules and priesthood, the idea of priestly authority and all religious dogmatism. It believed in the independence of each individual. We all have the responsibility for working out our own individual destiny.

Cârvâka philosophers taught that the world of the senses is the only real world. The only reality is that which we perceive with our minds through the five senses. So matter or nature is all. When elements combine to form a body, the spirit also comes into existence. When the body dies the spirit goes with it. This life is the only life we have. There is no supernatural world and no life after death. Nothing exists after the death of the body. There is no such thing as a soul and karma is an illusion.

Cârvâka philosophers argued that since this is the only life we have we should enjoy it to the full. So, unlike so much religious teaching, the Cârvâka was thoroughly life-affirming and had no hesitation in encouraging people to enjoy the sensual pleasures of life.

Hedonistic philosophies are always condemned as irresponsible by those who cannot understand the idea of life as something joyful. Sometimes there is justification in that condemnation. Hedonism has always suffered because of the irresponsibility of some hedonists. But there was no irresponsibility in the teaching of the Cârvâka philosophers. They understood that true joy is to be found in making a full and positive contribution to the life of society. Like modern Humanism, their atheism was naturalistic and life-affirming in a way which managed to be both responsible and joyous.

The other two forms of atheism in India to which I wish to refer are quite different. Like Taoism in China, they both speak to the hearts and minds of those who like to say, 'I am not religious but I am spiritual'. The two are Jainism and Buddhism. Both of them have emerged from Hinduism.

Jainism seems to have begun as a simple, austere, atheistic reforming movement within Hinduism. It was strongly critical of the Brahmin priesthood and of the caste system as a whole and its literature contains many attacks on the Hindu belief in gods.

But Jainism retained the Hindu belief in the karmic cycle of births and rebirths. It developed primarily as a very simple and extremely demanding ascetic path of escape from that cycle. Each individual is regarded as responsible for his or her own fate. Escape from the karmic cycle is achieved by following a pathway of ethical living which leads us away from attachment to our earthly lives and all the baggage that goes with them. Through non-attachment, escape from the cycle of lives finally becomes possible and we find lasting happiness and ultimate bliss.

The ethical code includes five vows, many of which will seem very familiar. The vow not to kill is much more than that simple negative might suggest. It involves a deep respect for all living things. The second and third vows are not to lie and not to steal. The fourth is celibacy but not quite celibacy as we know it. For Jaina monks celibacy is virtually the same vow as that taken by Roman Catholic priests. But for the laity it simply means the observation of the principle of monogamy – complete faithfulness to one partner.

The last vow is the renunciation of pleasure in material things. This is the vow which can lead us away from attachment to the things of this world and so to escape from the cycle of karma. It begins with an attitude of detachment towards all of our material possessions and ends in our release from the cycle of reincarnation.

Buddhism is far better known in the west than either of the two systems of unbelief that I have mentioned so far. It began with a rejection of all speculation about gods and with opposition both to the Brahmin priesthood and to the caste system. But it retained the Hindu concept of life bound within a karmic cycle involving a series of re-births to new lives on earth.

Like Jainism, Buddhism teaches that it is by our own initiative and effort that we escape back into the All which is Ultimate Reality.

Both Jainism and Buddhism share a doctrine of non-violence and respect for life, so when we see Buddhists involved in violence it becomes clear that, like the rest of us, fundamental beliefs go by the board when we are under pressure.

Gautama Siddhartha, born about 563 BCE was the founder of Buddhism. To him, life is a recurring cycle of suffering and death caused by desire. In order to enable us to escape into nirvana, Gautama developed his teaching of the four noble truths and the eightfold path. This leads through enlightenment to nirvana, a state of being where suffering and death no longer exist.

Perhaps the simplest way for an outsider to look at Buddhism it to look at 'The Three Signs of Being'; 'The Four Noble Truths'; and 'The Noble Eight-fold Path'.

The Three Signs of Being

These three characteristics form the basis of Buddhist philosophy. They are called the three signs of Being.

The first is that all is change or impermanence.

The second is that all is suffering.

And the third is that all is One.

Thus there is no ultimate individuality and the self has no ultimate separateness. The self must be freed from bondage to itself so that it may be merged with the All.

The Four Noble Truths

These truths are derived from the three signs of Being. They have to do with suffering and desire.

The first is that suffering is the disease which needs a cure.

The second is that suffering is caused by desire.

The word desire has a very much wider meaning when used in this context than it does in our normal usage. It covers the whole craving of human beings for personal fulfilment and satisfaction. It covers everything involved in our struggle to cling to our own individuality and our own identity. These are the things that bind us to the Wheel of Rebirth. It follows that:

The third noble truth is that the elimination of desire will remove the cause of man-made suffering.

The fourth noble truth is optimistic. There IS a way of escape from the Wheel of Rebirth. Desire can be eliminated through the noble eight-fold path.

The Noble Eight-fold Path

The eight-fold path consists of right views, right motives, right speech, right action, right livelihood, right effort, right concentration and right awareness. Some of these require further comment.

Right views or understanding involves an intellectual grasp of the three signs of being, the four noble truths, the nature of the self and the law of karma.

In our growth towards a right attitude of mind or right motives there are three stages. First there is the recognition that it pays to be moral because moral living leads to happiness and immoral living to pain. This is 'the crime doesn't pay' stage.

This is followed by the state of reason. Reason teaches us that moral living affects other people's lives in beneficial ways and immoral living in harmful ways, so we choose morality for the sake of others.

Finally, morality is chosen because virtue is its own reward.

In spite of the fact that every element of the Buddhist path is defined with the greatest care, I can by-pass right speech and move on to right conduct or action. This is defined in terms of five precepts.

The first is to refrain from injury to living things. The true Buddhist believes in non-violence and has a reverence for all living things.

The second precept is to refrain from taking that which is not given.

Then Buddhists are to exercise self-control in regard to sex; they are to refrain from falsehood; and they are to refrain from taking alcohol or drugs.

These five precepts prepare the way for charity, the practice of kindliness and helpfulness in thought, word and deed. By following these precepts which all together make up right conduct, the Buddhist acquires merit which is of value on the road to enlightenment.

Next in the noble eightfold path is right livelihood. When I was a young Methodist I remember discussions in Sunday School on questions of Christian Citizenship.

Should a Christian drink alcohol even in moderation? Should a Christian gamble? Should a Christian work in drink-related or gambling-related businesses: breweries, pubs, pools offices, betting shops and so on. This kind of question tends only to raise more questions which become increasingly finicky and precious. But it is the kind of question which Buddhists will understand. For when they talk about right livelihood they mean that our occupation must be compatible with the five precepts of right conduct and with all the other parts of the noble eightfold path.

The prize of enlightenment is only for those who strive with diligence – right effort. The nature of our striving is itself clearly defined in four ways:

We are to strive to prevent new evil entering the mind;
to remove all evil that is already there;
to develop all good that is already in the mind;
and to acquire still more unceasingly.

Which brings us to the two final elements: right concentration and right awareness or right meditation or serenity. Having acquired some degree of moral and physical control the Buddhist begins to approach the control and evolution of the mind; the control of thought.

Right awareness is awareness of the still centre of the turning world. It is mind-development carried to heights beyond our normal understanding and it is the gateway to wisdom and compassion. When awareness is merged with wisdom and compassion the individual knows its oneness with the All and becomes free: free from the fetters of ignorance, free from the snares of desire and of self. He is on the threshold of nirvana, ready to be lost in the All.

I have felt it necessary to spend time with these three systems of ethics because none of them requires any religious beliefs at all. They give the lie to the oft-made claim that you can't have ethics without religion.

14

China

Before the advent of communism, three systems of thought gave an intellectual and ethical basis to the life of one of the most populous areas of the world – an area which has also been one of the most stable in all the world: China.

Communism nowadays is mostly thought of in terms of political systems which have moved a very long way from the social and economic idealism of Karl Marx. At its best it has been the inspiration behind the lives and thinking of many highly intelligent and compassionate people. Except to note that it is an atheistic philosophy, I have no intention of studying it in these pages.

The three systems of thought and ethics which traditionally underpinned Chinese life were Confucianism and Taoism which were home grown; and Mahayana Buddhism which was imported.

Unlike the original Theravada Buddhism which we have already looked at, Mahayana Buddhism has reverted to a host of religious practices and ideas, taking into its embrace the practice of primitive societies it has influenced.

Like Theravada Buddhism, Taoism is another philosophy which can be very attractive to those who say 'I am not religious but I am spiritual.' It is perhaps the negative to Buddhism's positive. Buddhism speaks of ultimate reality as 'the All'. Taoism speaks of it as 'No-thing.' Having looked at Buddhism in some detail I shall pass over Taoism fairly rapidly later in this chapter. But I must give rather closer attention to the teachings of Confucius (born in either 552 or 551 BCE).

If Taoism can be defined as 'the Way' seeking harmony between the individual and the natural world; then Confucianism can be defined as 'the Way' seeking harmony between individual and individual within society.

Confucius was a very conservative thinker who began from the ideas and thinking of his own time and used them as the launch pad for his own thinking summed up in 'the Analects'.

In his time the spirits of nature were widely believed in. He made no attempt to get rid of that belief. Instead, he acknowledged the existence of the spirits of nature but paid no attention to them. They were of no interest to him.

He also took over the ancient concept of 'the Mandate of Heaven', the moral law and he took over the concept of tao, 'the Way'. But whereas Taoism claims that ultimately it is impossible to know, define or describe the Way, Confucius set out to do just that. He set out to examine the moral law and the Way and to spell them out so that anyone can know them and follow them.

This led to a teaching which is thoroughly this worldly, wholly centred upon man and society.

Confucius had no belief in life after death but felt that it doesn't matter anyway. Human affairs are all visible. We should devote our minds to what follows birth and precedes death because we cannot avoid the conduct of ordinary, everyday life. It is moral principle which determines how we should behave in ordinary life. So Confucius' teaching was directed at showing how life should be lived and how social relationships should be expressed. He taught a way of life in which morality occupies a supreme position.

Behind Confucius' pursuit of the ideal moral character lies the unspoken, and therefore unquestioned, assumption that the only purpose we can have, and also the only worthwhile thing we can do, is to become as good as we possibly can. Perhaps Confucius saw this as the ancient 'Decree of Heaven'.

Since in being moral we can neither be assured of a reward nor guaranteed success, morality must be pursued for its own sake. It is its own reward. The demands of morality are categorical and have no connection with self-interest at all. If need be we have to sacrifice even our life in doing what is right.

Human nature is morally neutral. How different this is from the Christian doctrine of original sin, and to my mind, how much more accurate as a picture of how human beings actually are. We begin life with a clean sheet like those old wax tablets on which children learned to write or draw. The ideal moral character is that of the person who has developed his character through sheer hard work. It is only by working at it that we become morally good.

This does not mean that when we fail we become overwhelmed with a sense of sin and riddled with guilt. Because Confucianism has no reference to a God or gods it has no sense of sin. The crucial thing is not whether we succeed or fail. What matters is that we are striving after virtue. If we are, we can put our failures behind us and try to rise above them. Self-recrimination and blame are pointless. When we fail we simply face up to what has happened and begin again. And the way to begin again is not to pursue self-interest but to pursue virtue – virtue for its own sake with no thought of either reward or worldly success.

Confucian teaching revolves around a number of important virtues such as benevolence, wisdom, courage, trustworthiness, moral seriousness and respectfulness. Benevolence is far and away the most important. It is the compassion which enables us to identify with the joys and troubles of others and it involves following the golden rule. Confucius was one of the first of many to come up with some form of the golden rule. He said, 'Do not impose on others what you yourself do not desire.'

When Confucius says that benevolence involves 'observing the rites' he simply means that we are to observe the traditionally accepted rules and customs by which private and social behaviour are regulated. This includes both the ordinary outward forms of social behaviour and the deeper questions of social morality. Many years ago, on the old P & O liner *The Canton*, I went to dinner wearing a sweater. I was sent back to my cabin to change into a jacket and tie. Nowadays most of us are a great deal more casual but in many parts of the world the outward forms are still observed with a good deal of care. Confucius felt that those outward forms were important, but only as the expression of our social and moral relationships and responsibilities. Those relationships and responsibilities begin at home. To Confucius, filial love and responsibility are supreme. Human love begins with the natural love and obligations between members of the same family, and it moves outward in decreasing degrees. Love for our fellow men and women is an extension of the love we have for the members of our own families.

The second Confucian virtue is wisdom or intelligence. It is this which gives us the ability to judge what is right and what is wrong. It is also this which enables us to judge the characters of other people and to become a good judge of character. To fail to do what is right when we know what it is, is to show a lack of courage.

Courage is the third Confucian virtue but it is not always a virtue. In the hands of the good, courage is a means to good but in the hands of the wicked, courage only increases the evil they will do. To be a virtue, courage must be in the service of morality and must be allied to benevolence. It is never enough to speak of any of these virtues in isolation. They all belong together.

And it is trustworthiness which helps to hold them together. The word translated trustworthiness has no exact equivalent in English but it includes trustworthiness, reliability and keeping faith. It means living up to one's word. It is therefore wise to be quick to act but slow to speak. When I was a boy I had a book of devotion which left one page free for people to write down their own pledges. I wrote, 'If I make none, I break none.'

I little knew it but that is very Confucian. The wise, good person is the person who makes few promises and keeps them, rather than the one who makes many promises and fails to keep them. As one of my cousins wrote in my childhood autograph album: 'It is better to do and not promise, than to promise and not do.'

Confucius' fifth virtue is variously translated 'serious-ness', 'reverence' or 'duty'. It combines the fear of failing in our responsibilities with a serious single-mindedness in the fulfilment of those responsibilities. And since our responsibilities are seen primarily in terms of social relationships, the sixth virtue is respectfulness, which describes our attitude to other people. It includes both etiquette and good manners and also the inner attitude of respect for other people. Etiquette and good manners are important because social order should be preserved as little as possible by force and as much as possible by custom.

Something apparently simple like respectfulness is important because it is something over which we have control. There are so many things in life over which we have no control. These are things (our destiny or fate if you like) which we just have to accept. There is no point in spending our energies complaining about them or fighting them or trying to change them. Acceptance leaves us free to bend all our endeavours to the pursuit of those things we can control: moral excellence or virtue.

Confucianism is primarily an ethic for the individual. Its social dimension lies in the influence virtuous people exert and in the service they give to the community. Confucius always had one eye on government service. The good Confucian would make an excellent civil servant, hard working, upstanding and incorruptible. Confucius was quite clear that it is only right to serve the state if we can do so without compromising our ideals. If the state upholds the tao, the Way, then we can serve the state. If not, then those of us in public service do better to retire.

So the Confucian is no unthinking patriot. S/he does not

believe 'my country right or wrong'. But s/he is not a revolutionary either. 'What goes around, comes around' and the Confucian is prepared to wait for better times, quietly getting on with life in the best possible way. So the Confucian is a quietist as also is the Taoist. Perhaps that helps to explain why Chinese society has been so stable over the centuries.

Although Confucius was thoroughly conservative in his approach, emphasising the importance of reverence towards the customs and the ancient codes of behaviour, he was no hidebound conservative. He urged respect for the ancient codes because they had all the authority of the moral thinking of the past, but they were not to be accepted without question. Rules are constantly in need of adaptation and change. Some become obsolete and new rules become necessary. And behind the rules there is always basic moral principle. It is the spirit behind the rules that counts, not the rules themselves. No moral system can be based solely either on rules or on virtues. So there is always a dialogue between rule and principle and it is this which constitutes the essence of Confucius' moral thinking. For him there were no absolutes.

So here we have another thoroughgoing ethical system which owes nothing to religion at all. It has stood the test of time and in its later developments has shown itself to be open to the scientific ways of thinking that have become so natural to us nowadays.

But the Taoist felt that Confucianism does not go far enough. Like modern humanism, it focussed entirely on human beings, on our lives as individuals and on our interpersonal relationships. Taoism sought to set all of this within the framework of our place in the natural world and even beyond this; the spiritual world which is beyond our understanding.

The taoist claimed with some justification that in spelling things out in such detail, Confucius becomes restrictive and ties people down. Ethical systems are all very well in their way but they can easily lead to a kind of sense of moral superiority – something which Jesus condemned in the Pharisees and something which many of us condemn in the more modern Puritans and in the 19th century Nonconformist Conscience.

Jesus once painted a lovely picture of the man who prayed, 'God I thank thee that I am not as other men are' and then went on to tell God what a wonderful man he was!

Confucius would have been the first to condemn 'holier than thou' attitudes but there is no doubt that his kind of ethical system can lead people to *think* of themselves as Superior and Noble Minded, instead of actually becoming noble minded and first class human beings.

One great Taoist was wonderfully mocking about the value of ethics. Chuang Tzu claimed that if you want to hear the very best speeches on love, duty, justice and so on all you have to do is to listen to politicians. They have learned that the more you pile up ethical principles and duties and obligations to bring everyone into line the more you gather loot for those who rule over you.

He also claimed that there is a sense in which ethical systems are entirely unnecessary. Most people are honest and reliable without realising it. They love each other without ever thinking that they are obeying a law which says that they must. They are honest, trustworthy and reliable without having to think about these things. They live freely with one another, generous and always ready to help each other without ever having to be told that this is the right way to live.

So, instead of tying ourselves down with rules and customs and ethical systems, we need to keep ourselves open. Thus far the unbeliever will probably travel with the Taoist. For the unbeliever simply wants us to remain open and flexible so that we can face each new challenge as it comes, without preconceived or fixed ideas.

But the Taoist is not quite as open as that. He wants us to be open to the guidance of the divine Tao, the cosmic Tao, the source of all good, the No-Thing that cannot be defined. Although in practical terms there probably isn't that much difference between the two positions, as I said at the beginning of this chapter, Taoism takes us back into the realm of those who like to claim, 'I am not religious but I am spiritual.'

e

15

Ancient Greece

In this book so far I have chosen to write about religious belief systems and then about systems of unbelief. What should have been perfectly clear from the start is that belief and unbelief have always existed side by side. Even in such a theocratic state as ancient Israel there were those 'fools' who said in their hearts 'there is no God' (see the Psalms).

There have been times when religion has been powerful enough to persecute and silence the alternatives. That has been particularly true of Christianity and Islam and the reverse has been true of some communist states. But the alternatives have always been there and as soon as it has become possible they have surfaced again and made themselves heard, seen and felt.

But as we turn to ancient Greece we find city states, so open and vibrant that a host of competing and mutually exclusive religious and non-religious philosophical and ethical systems flourished side by side.

When the Christian Church became politically powerful

it did its best to destroy some of these teachings. In some of the worst acts of vandalism the world has ever seen, great libraries, such as the one at Alexandria, were destroyed. But thanks in part to Moslem scholars and in large part to the Renaissance, where so much was rediscovered and preserved, we now know a good deal about many of these ancient systems of unbelief.

Ancient Greek religion was pretty primitive, with a host of gods and a wonderful array of myths and legends. As in so much else, it is Homer who gives us our most vivid and thoughtful picture of that religion.

The gods of Homer are human! Elsewhere they became a mixture of fantasy, sometimes animals and birds and sometimes demonic. But in Greece the supreme interest was the human being and so the gods were human too. What is more, they were neither more nor less moral than humans. There were many horrible ancient myths about the gods but Homer cleansed his gods of the horror. He painted them as humans blown up to a larger scale and set on a larger canvas. Their behaviour was thoroughly human. As Dorothea Wender put it, 'They lie, cheat, steal, manhandle each other, play favourites and commit adultery rather more than Homer's humans do.'

But behind the gods there is another power which the gods can strain but which they cannot break. This is the power which represents the rhythm of the universe. Both the gods and humans are subject to that rhythm and to the law of cause and effect. And yet, within our fixed destiny there is still enough elasticity to allow a measure of personal freedom. There are real choices we can make. So, in Homer's Iliad, Achilles has the choice between staying at home in Greece and enjoying a long life or going to Troy, respected and honoured by his fellows but risking an early death.

And of course, the very fact that there are so many gods, ensures that humans have considerable freedom of action. For the gods have their own favourites and are on different sides. In Homer's story, some favour the Greeks and some favour the Trojans. They also have lives of their own, so at crucial times in the affairs of men, they may well have better things to do than to bother with what is going on on earth. And sometimes when they do want to intervene in our affairs, Zeus (their father) won't allow them to.

But there is something else, and my boarding school headmaster can point the way. He was an old school disciplinarian so we were always being caned or, for lesser offences, scatted (beaten with a gym shoe). I'm not sure how much he discussed things with his colleagues but he certainly had and exercised the power of Zeus in the school. Every so often he would come up with some new idea which was imposed by dictat and became law. But many of us felt that some of his ideas were crack-brained, or if not that, certainly not things that should become compulsory.

If any of us had the guts to go and confront him, to stand up to him and to refuse to accept his new rules, we would win his admiration and support, and sometimes even persuade him into concessions.

Homer shows that the same is true of our relationship with the gods of ancient Greece. Because the gods are human, ordinary humans can influence them. If people are noble enough and have sufficient courage, they can stand up to the gods and win their admiration and support.

I have loved Homer's stories ever since I was introduced to them as a six-year-old council school boy by one of our teachers. Before I move on from him I want to draw attention to some of the things that mattered most to him, things which were to go on having a major impact on the thought and life of ancient Greece, and things which were to become important in the life and culture of Great Britain at the height of her power and influence.

Homer saw life in terms of this life, from birth to death. Within that framework he was always life-affirming. He displayed a great respect for tradition and the home. Modern women will not be satisfied with his approach to women who were seen above all as mothers and home-makers but it is the respect Homer shows that is the heart of his attitudes. He shows respect to women, even when we may feel that they don't deserve it; he is respectful towards servants, towards the elderly, even towards enemies. He shows that people deserve respect, not for any status they may have in society, but for the kind of people they are.

Homer believed that the home should be a place of hospitality – the kind of hospitality you find in traditional societies but which is largely dead in cultures like our own. He loved freedom and peace and believed that we should seek the common good – even the good of our enemies. He delighted in beauty including physical beauty; had a great love for life; believed in moderation in all things and yet set as his supreme human goal the quest of an excellence which includes a sense of moral responsibility.

It is difficult to pin down everything we find in Homer: clarity of thought, insight, realism, honesty, toleration and moderation. There is also a great love for freedom and for peace. Freedom is no individual thing. It includes freedom of speech and it involves striving for the common good and that really does mean the good of everybody. After we have battled with our enemies, peace treaties need to seek the good of our enemies as well as of ourselves, which is why old men who could see the whole picture were called in to work the treaties out. Greek ideals of democracy arose from such ideas.

Running through the whole of Homer's approach to life is the ideal of excellence. Closely linked with it is his love of beauty. Whether in gods, men or women, beauty is honoured. It is this which inspired generations of artists and sculptors. And it is also this love of beauty which made the Greek approach to the human body so different from anything in the Judaeo-Christian and later the Moslem world. Sadly it was an approach rejected by influential Plato but these early Ionian Greeks enjoyed the beauty of the human body without embarrassment and without fear.

Above all there is a great love for life, a great zest for life. Believing that this life is the only one that has any real meaning, they felt that they had to live it to the full by striving for excellence in every part of life. Successs or failure was irrelevant. Provided people strive for excellence they deserve to be honoured. In striving for excellence we find true joy and so receive the rewards of virtue in this life. For ancient Greeks, Homer's Odysseus was perhaps their greatest model, 'so civilised, so intelligent, so self-possessed' as the goddess Athene put it – but also a man of genuine modesty.

Homer then, was very much more than just a story-teller and his influence has been incalculable. His passions and ideals remain of lasting value and attractiveness. They form the base from which Greek thought moved on.

16

Glimpses of the Future

We have seen that Homer is the starting point for all Greek thought. From him we have derived the ideal of all-round excellence. Humans are seen whole and must strive to be the best that they can be.

There is no division yet between religion and irreligion. The most typical feature of the Greek mind thus far is a sense of the wholeness of things. There is no distinction between the body and the soul, the physical and the spiritual. There is simply the whole person and education was aimed at training the whole person.

All that is about to change. After Homer, two new philosophical approaches began to represent two main strands of thought – strands which also represent the most typical and deepest division in all of human thought and practice.

The strand which has been best preserved and best known is the one which derives from Orphism, Pythagoras, Socrates and Plato. That this philosophical strand has been so well preserved is partly due to the greatness of its advocates, but also because it could be made compatible with the Christian religion. In combination with Christianity and blessed with political power, it became completely dominant in Europe until the Renaissance.

According to Plato, nature is the product of a designing Mind. Man's task is to study and follow nature and to fulfil the divine design. Plato saw man as a divided creature comprising body and mind or soul. The body is mortal but the mind has the capacity for immortality. All this is far removed from the Homeric conception of man as a single whole and it is far removed from his ideal of the excellence of the whole person. That ideal was very much better preserved by the proponents of the other main philosophical approach of the time. This strand was not religious. Mostly it was not religious in the sense that it ignored religion without fighting over it. Agnostic about the gods, it simply assumed that if there were any gods they would have no interest in us and so we didn't need to have any interest in them.

But there were plenty of people who were prepared to go much further. Xenophanes, who was himself a religious philosopher, mocked the anthropomorphism of traditional ideas: 'Men believe that the gods are clothed and shaped and speak like themselves. If oxen and horses and lions could draw and paint, they would delineate the gods in their own image.'

Even more bluntly, the playwright Euripides wrote, 'There are no gods in heaven. To believe such is to believe old wives' tales and is stupid.'

So there was an agnosticism which for all practical purposes lived life without reference to religion or the gods and there was a more vigorous atheism which even then managed to provoke the Athenian authorities into laws against atheism. The old irrational fears have a long history.

I want to glance briefly at just a few of these thinkers.

It is astonishing how modern some of their ideas sound and it is remarkable how up to date many of their ideas were. After their work was lost, buried or banned, it took us nearly two thousand years to rediscover many of the things they thought or knew. In the period between about 600 and 400 BCE a number of Ionian thinkers carried forward an approach to nature which is very similar to our own. Instead of treating nature as divine or filling it with gods and spirits, they tried to understand it and to discover how it works.

They combined observation, experiment and reason in their attempt to understand the fundamental elements of the universe. Their approach was an expression of their sense of wonder, their curiosity and their desire to know. It was matched by their firm belief in the power of human reason. They started from the assumption that the universe is law abiding and therefore capable of explanation. Thanks to Thales, the first of these thinkers, they also assumed that the universe is one whole. I want to refer to just one or two of them, beginning with Anaximander who was probably born just before 600 BCE.

He began from the assumption that the present complexity of the universe evolved from something simpler. Noticing the fact that where other animal babies quickly become self-sufficient, human children need a long period of suckling, and making a careful study of the smooth shark, he developed a primitive form of evolutionary theory.

He suggested that all living creatures arose from water and that man was originally a fish and developed through the animals and from them.

Anaximander's view that evolution moves from the simple to the complex was in line with the general Greek idea that the universe must not only be rational and knowable but also simple because truth is simple. The apparent multiplicity of physical things, the apparent variety and richness of life, these are superficial appearances. Underlying them all is an essential simple unity.

In modern times it was a long time before Darwin's *Origin of Species* finally began to establish the evolutionary facts. What began the modern scientific revolution was a completely different field of study: astronomy. It was people like Copernicus and Galileo who set their particular cats among the pigeons.

But way back in 480 or 479 BCE a thinker called Anaxagoras settled in Athens. Although some of his ideas remained very primitive, he moved forward our understanding of the sun, the moon and the stars. He was the first to explain that the moon shines by reflected light and he also explained the nature of eclipses. The Babylonians had learned to predict eclipses but it took Anaxagoras to explain them.

Medicine was another field in which the Greeks began to prize open the door towards a rational and scientific approach. Everybody has heard of Hippocrates, born in Cos in 460 BCE, and of the Hippocratic oath – and no, doctors are not required to sign up to it, although it does set out some pretty fine principles on which medical workers can usefully direct their lives and their relationships with patients.

During Hippocrates' life he belonged to the guild of physicians called Asclepiadae. The collection of books that bears his name is a collection written by a number of different authors over a period of perhaps three hundred years. It is in the book called *The Sacred Disease* that the scene is set for a new scientific approach to medicine by these ancient Greeks. In it, the author claims that 'primitive man regards everything he cannot explain as the word of a god.' That is why epilepsy was called 'the sacred disease'. Our author wrote:

It is not more divine or more sacred than other diseases, but has a natural cause, and its supposed divine origin is due to men's inexperience, and to their wonder at its peculiar character. My own view is that those who first attributed a sacred character to this malady were like the magicians, purifiers, charlatans and quacks of our own day, men who claim great piety and superior knowledge. Being at a loss, and having no treatment which would help, they concealed and sheltered themselves behind superstition, and called this illness sacred, in order that their utter ignorance might not be manifest. . . Should the patient recover, they claim the credit, 'but should he die. . . they are not at all to blame, but the gods.

But this disease is in my opinion no more divine than any other; it has the same nature as other diseases. . . It is also curable. . .

These ancient Greeks began to see that medicine should be

based on accurate observation and the gathering together of accumulated experience. Sadly, their ideas and the reaching forward to modern medical science which they offered were lost to the philosophic/religious approach to medicine and had to wait for the Renaissance before they re-emerged. In Renaissance times the church was still forbidding the kinds of research that medicine needed if it was to make progress.

Needless to say, medicine and surgery have moved on a long way since Hippocrates' day, although there wasn't much advance until quite modern times. But some of the principles behind Hippocrates' thinking and the kind of ethical approach he brought to his work still have plenty to say to us.

When we were looking at religion there were times when I had to be highly selective. Otherwise this book would have become an encyclopedia! For example, we looked at none of the four great monotheisms.

The same has to be true when we look at unbelief. And often, it will seem as though we are not really talking about unbelief at all. Often, the people I am writing about were simply people who put religion on the back burner, not denying it but treating it as an irrelevance. Whatever their personal beliefs that was often wise. Charges of atheism could lead to exile as they did with the Sophist Protagoras who was so much admired by Socrates; or they could lead to death as they did in the case of Socrates himself.

I don't propose to look at the Sophists or the Cynics or the Sceptics, all of them groups containing men whose unbelief was vigorous and clear. Nor do I propose to look at the religious wing of Greek thought exemplified in

Plato and in the Stoics. Selective though it is, I propose only to look at two important paths. The first runs from the fourth century BCE philosopher Democritus to Epicurus and beyond. And secondly, I wish to focus on Aristotle and his book on 'Ethics'.

17

Democritus, Epicurus and Lucretius

None of our thinking is done in a vacuum. Democritus was born in about 460 BCE in Abdera, home of the famous sophist Protagoras. Democritus, a vigorous and cheerful philosopher, took an early atomic theory of the composition of the universe which had been developed by Leucippus of Miletus (c.500-440 BCE) and made it the basis of all his teaching. He founded a school in Abdera and believed that all reality consisted of basic atomic structures existing in a void.

So he and his followers taught that being does not come to be or perish. It simply IS. Being is an infinite number of atoms in space constantly grouping and regrouping. Thus the world and the stars and planets are simply temporary groups of atoms. And human beings are also temporary groups which will disperse at death and enter into new groupings.

Democritus rejected popular religion. The gods were either the creation of man's imagination or, if they really existed, they were temporary groups of atoms just like us.

Democritus was a strict determinist who believed that everything that happens, happens in accordance with natural laws. He was a thorough-going materialist whose goal in life was cheerfulness achieved through moderation and culture. He disliked passion and violence and distrusted the senses, so he valued friendship but not sexual love. His ethics sprang from his reliance on reason and his ethical goal was peace of mind, an untroubled calm derived from a rational knowledge of the nature of things.

Democritus' greatest disciple was Epicurus. It is said that Epicurus never acknowledged his debt to Democritus. If that is true, then it is a serious criticism of him. But there was so much hostility to Epicurus, first from the Stoics and then from the early Christians (who saw him as a threat) that very little of his own writing has survived and we are largely dependent upon Lucretius, a Roman disciple of Epicurus for what we know of Epicureanism. Almost all copies of Lucretius' work were lost or destroyed so we were nearly left with nothing. All of which means that we don't actually know whether Epicurus acknowledged his debt to Democritus or not.

What we do know is that there is no ancient teacher who has been more consistently misunderstood, misrepresented and maligned than Epicurus. This is particularly unfortunate because his was a teaching of great simplicity and warm humanity.

Epicurus was the son of an Athenian colonist and was born in 342 or 341 BCE in Samos. When he was a boy, all Athenians were turned out of Samos and Epicurus and his family lived in exile – there is some uncertainty about where. In 311 BCE he founded a school in Mitylene. A year later he moved the school to Lampsacus and in 307 BCE he moved it to Athens. Here he bought a house and a large garden where he established his philosophical community, what has been called his 'society of friends'.

Given his reputation, carefully built up by his critics from that day to this, the real facts of his life and work are astounding. HE LIVED QUIETLY AND ABSTEMIOUSLY. He achieved a kind of philosophical nobility, even saintliness, in spite of the fact that for years he suffered great pain from a bowel complaint. He was loved and revered by his followers.

If we look at his followers we see a pioneer not simply ahead of his own time but amazingly, still ahead of ours! He taught adults and children, Greeks and foreigners (most of them from the Greek cities of Asia Minor), women and slaves. Pythagoras and Plato had both been to some degree pioneers of women's rights but it was Epicurus who took foreigners, women, slaves and children into his community all on equal terms. It was Epicurus who gave equal standing to everyone no matter what their race, sex or social position. It was Epicurus who welcomed prostitutes as people rather than as bodies to be exploited and used.

Christians are often rightly proud of the way Jesus treated social outcasts, yet in its attitude to women and its dealings with women, Christianity still has a long way to go before it catches up with Epicurus. And society at large has a very long way to go before it even begins to show people the kind of respect Epicurus gave them, regardless of their nationality, status or background.

The only earlier philosophy of which Epicurus made

much use was that of Democritus and the Ionian Atomists. He combined the old Ionian interest in nature with his moral concerns. He found in the atomism of Democritus a philosophy which destroyed fear of the gods and an unpleasant afterlife. He believed that the philosophy of Democritus would bring peace and self-reliance. As soon as reason begins to reveal the true nature of the universe, the terrors which have haunted the mind vanish. Knowledge of the world and our place in it takes all fear away.

The disciples he gathered around him lived simple, quiet, austere lives completely at odds with the pictures painted of them. The 'refreshments' he provided consisted largely of such basics as bread and water! They were not politically motivated, feeling rather that it was better to keep your heads down and to try to live well no matter what the political system under which you lived. So they were quietists of the highest moral character with an extraordinary devotion to their founder. For them, the supreme quality in life was the quality of human friendship. The whole of their theory and practice was built on strong and loyal friendship.

Epicurus himself lived simply and happily and was gentle and kindly, except perhaps towards other philosophers. He could be scathing about some of them. But in his own teaching he offered a commonsense approach to life and looked for a moral way of life which could produce peace of mind.

Virtually the whole of his teaching would have been lost but for the Roman poet Lucretius who wrote a poem expounding the atomic theory of Democritus and the teaching of Epicurus (published in about 55 BCE).

To Lucretius, these teachings came with all the force of a conversion experience. He joined those who dismissed metaphysical abstractions, divine providence and the immortal soul as vain illusions. Rationalist by temperament, he believed that these teachings disposed once and for all of all the bogeys which have frightened people through time. He found ample grounds for wonder and joy in the perceptible world and in the workings of natural law. The teachings of Epicurus enabled people to leave their fears behind, to accept the realities of human life and so to find happiness, peace and tranquillity.

In essence, Epicureanism is the simplest of all philosophies. It is a rule of life based on reason. Reason frees us from fear: fear of the gods or fear of death. And it is reason which keeps the emotions under control and so enables us to find that peace and tranquillity.

Epicureanism is often criticised for its emphasis on human happiness but there is widespread (and deliberate) misunderstanding. Epicureans did not believe that the way to happiness is through whipping up artificial pleasures to satisfy artificial demands. And they made the same distinction Aristotle made between pleasures of the moment and happiness as a permanent condition of life.

Epicurus believed that the way to happiness lay in living a simple, unpretentious life without luxury or extravagance, and also in being content with our lot as mortals. When we accept the simple fact that this life is all we have, we can get on with enjoying it simply and happily without any anxiety or fear about some unknown life beyond the grave. There is no point in pining for what cannot be or fearing what will not be.

If this life is the only one we have, then the greatest

good of all is the possession of life itself. We should aim to make that life as pleasant as it can be and the way to that kind of pleasure is through human friendship. Friendship lay at the heart of Epicurean teaching and communal life. It was central to the teaching of Epicurus himself. He was an intensely friendly man himself and believed that without friendship we cannot live well.

Through their very simple way of life, Epicureans tried to keep their fate in their own hands, to live a full and contented life and to die in peace. In place of ambition and the hunger for power, they offered the immediacy of true friends whose friendship would bring happiness. They believed that true happiness leads to the attainment of peace or imperturbable tranquillity. Ideally life is lived without pain, trouble or fear. Epicureans believed that their teachings could banish fear; that friendship could overcome trouble; and in the life of their founder they discovered that even long-term pain cannot take away our tranquillity. He bore his pain with the utmost courage and cheerfulness.

Although there are some pretty obvious deficiencies and weaknesses in the teaching of Epicurus, this remains for me one of the simplest, loveliest and most satisfying of all non-religious philosophies. I would go much further than that and say that, for me, together with the teachings of the Cârvâka philosophers of India, it is one of the most satisfying of all – full stop!

18

Aristotle

Aristotle was born in Stageira in Macedonia in 384 BCE. When he was eighteen he went to Athens to study under Plato at the Academy. He remained there until Plato's death and was perhaps Plato's greatest pupil. He always retained a great respect for his teacher but he was in no way Plato's disciple. A real polymath, he was too great a thinker in his own right to be anyone's disciple and he was not afraid to cross swords with his master. He was the kind of 'renaissance man' of all round interests and all round excellence such as the Greeks loved, and he turned his mind to a vast range of philosophical and scientific subjects.

After Plato's death in 347 BCE he left Athens, travelled, married, became tutor to Alexander the Great and in about 334 BCE he returned to Athens and founded the Lyceum, a school which was to last for five hundred years. Over the next ten years he studied, taught and wrote books on logic, metaphysics, theology, history, politics, ethics, aesthetics, psychology, anatomy, biology, zoology, botany, astronomy, meteorology, physics and chemistry! No wonder Bertrand Russell said that it was two thousands years before the world produced any philosopher who could be regarded as approximately his equal.

After the death of Alexander the Great, Aristotle's connection with him was remembered against him and he was charged with atheism. The charge was untrue. Aristotle believed in god as eternal mind, the unmoved mover and final cause. He thought of god as perfect and claimed that a perfect being can only think about perfection and therefore can only think of himself! He has no concern with us at all. But though the charge was untrue, Aristotle felt that discretion was the better part of valour and fled into exile to Chalcis in Euboea where he died that same year 322 BCE.

His ethics remain important for a number of reasons. First of all they are human, the work of a thoughtful human being. So they are not laws or commandments and they are not unchangeable. Human ideas can be rejected, revised and developed by rational argument and experience and they can be adjusted to the changing circumstances of human life.

On the other hand, because ethics is 'the study of what is right and good in conduct', its *essentials* do not change with the passing of time.

But although that is true, relativism is important in ethics. One of the religious criticisms still laid at the door of unbelievers is that they have no set of absolute, true and universal principles. The unbeliever will reply that there is no such thing. Universal principles have a nasty habit of coming unstuck just when life's questions and problems are becoming important.

Aristotle began with the claim that all our activities are geared to an end. The supreme end is the Good. It is therefore important for the conduct of our lives to know what the Good is, for the Good is that for the sake of which everything else is done. It is the goal of all of our actions. And Aristotle claimed that that end is happiness.

I don't think that he was right – how dare I say so! My own view is that happiness is a by-product of all sorts of other things – but I must stick with Aristotle for a while.

Happiness is more than pleasure – more even than a constant succession of pleasures. What is more, we can take *pleasure* both in things that are good and in things that are bad, and since Happiness is the Good, only the pleasures of goodness can lead to Happiness.

Happiness must also be distinguished from amusement or having a good time. Amusement is for relaxation. Happiness is not 'for' anything. It is itself the end. Happiness involves a sense of general well-being and fulfilment. It involves learning how to live successful and fulfilled human lives and therefore it involves virtue because to the good man virtuous activity is more desirable than anything else.

So happiness is achieved when life manages to combine virtue, goodness and all round excellence. It is simply a matter of always being the best that we can be. All of this involves moral responsibility. Both virtue and vice lie within our own power. It is in our power to do what is right and it is in our own power to do what is wrong. It is the regular choice of one or the other which ends up by making us either a good or a bad person.

Our task is to become good – to achieve the highest human good. Moral good is the result of habitual choice and leads to Happiness. And that involves the pursuit of virtue. But there are two kinds of virtue. There is intellectual virtue which begins with instruction and needs time and experience. And there is moral virtue which is the result of habitual choice. Both lead to Happiness. So we need the right kind of instruction and we need consistently to be making the right choices.

Ethical living is therefore active. It is a means of facing life and choosing the way we will live. And for Aristotle that meant choosing a middle way between extremes. The doctrine of the mean or middle way is perhaps the best remembered element in Aristotle's ethics and it is characteristically Greek. By nature passionate and excitable, they sought control and balance. If a violin string is too loose or too tight it gives the wrong notes and sounds awful. It only gives the right note if the tension is perfect.

This doctrine of the middle way has often led people to criticise Aristotle for a lack of passion. But perhaps all ethical systems are designed by the middle aged partly as an attempt to control the passions of the young. Just as many ethical systems seem to be either an attempt by the weak to keep the strong in check or an attempt by the wealthy to keep the poor in their place.

Aristotle recognised that finding the middle way is not easy. To do it well and consistently is a rare and praiseworthy achievement. But the doctrine of the mean is not universally applicable. There are some things which are always quite simply right and others which are also quite simply wrong.

It is when Aristotle begins to spell out his list of virtues that we really begin to find ourselves in trouble. Some of them have been severely criticised, sometimes because they deserve criticism and sometimes because people have not translated them into English with sufficient thought or understanding.

Fortunately it is not my task to attempt-to expound his list of virtues or the detail of his book. The book shows a man of towering intellect wrestling with the ordinary views and standards of his time, and trying to work out what should be the views of someone aiming at Goodness.

They demonstrate the childlike Greek delight in being human, a delight which surfaces again in Renaissance Italy. There is no false modesty here but only praise for greatness of spirit and generosity of spirit. Traditional attitudes to forgiveness and revenge are examined in the light of the virtuous man's quest for goodness. There is a great deal about friendship.

Aristotle also studies justice and injustice, equity and fair play and he spends a good deal of time with what he calls the intellectual virtues – virtues which do not come naturally to us but which have to be taught and which lead to what Aristotle calls the noblest human activity of all, the contemplation of perfection.

Inevitably perhaps, there are times when he displays something of the sense of superiority of the intellectual over the rest of us, but all of his studies are geared to enabling us to find the path to human happiness, and they rest on the conviction that it is virtue and the virtuous life which lead to happiness.

All of this has demonstrated very forcibly my main

f

contention that ethics stands on its own. It doesn't need a religion or divine authority or authentication. Indeed, it is all the better without religion because religionless ethics is more flexible and more open to change in the face of changing human circumstances and new human problems – the sort of problems new science is throwing up all the time.

19

The Inadequacy of Ethics

I have suggested elsewhere in these pages that ethical systems are sometimes devised by the weak in an attempt to protect themselves from the strong; they are sometimes devised by the wealthy in an attempt to protect themselves from the poor and needy; and they are sometimes designed by the elderly who are worried about the passions of the young. And it is the elderly, whose ethical systems and values are often so wonderfully fine, who demonstrate most vividly the inadequacy of ethics.

Ethical systems are based on our human experience of life as it is and on our ability to think about how it should be. They set out to show us the values and goals we should aim for. They set out to encapsulate all that we mean by 'the good life', a life that is satisfying and fulfilling and a life that will lead to the deepest experiences of happiness and contentment. Using human experience and the gift of reason we set out to show how best we can make the most and the best of the life we have.

So they have much to teach us but they all have the

same fatal weakness. *They can show us how to live but they cannot enable us.* For none of them takes into account the human emotions and passions. All the sensible, lofty ethical teaching in the world cannot save us from our passions. When those are roused they can lift us into the most supremely magical moments of our lives. But they can also act like a tsunami, sweeping away all the defences which the most faithful of us have tried to build and leaving a trail of destruction and devastation.

It is that particular problem which St. Paul wrestles with in his letter to the Romans (chapters 5 ff). Paul talks about the inner conflict we endure when we want to do what is right but we also want to do what is wrong, and the desire for wrongdoing seems to be more powerful than the desire to do what is right.

And it is just at that moment that the power of reason will let us down. It is reason that has established the set of values by which we live and the goals we seek to attain. But now, passion takes over our reason and leads us to rationalise in favour of the wrongdoing that has become so attractive to us. It is amazing how easy it is to find good reasons for cooking the books at work; for misusing a business expenses account; for petty theft. And it is amazing how easy it is to find good reasons for committing adultery, or if not good reasons, at least good excuses! Wherever there is a desirable wrong, our reason will help us to justify it.

Which leaves us with what seems to be an inescapable conundrum. We know the way to live. But we don't live that way because we desire other things.

If we reach crisis point; if we are left after the tsunami facing the wreckage of our lives; is there any way forward? There are two.

There is the path spelt out by St. Paul. It is a path other religions would recognise and approve and spell out in their different ways according to their own traditions. It is the path of utter and complete surrender. When we are at rock bottom and our lives are bankrupt, we turn to our Lord and Saviour and give our lives into the hands of that Saviour. 'I am no longer my own, but thine.' We place our lives in the hands of our Saviour and give up all responsibility for those lives. From that moment we will simply 'trust and obey' because for us there really is 'no other way'.

At this point I find myself considerably torn. I have no desire to undermine or undervalue that path for those who feel that it is the right path for them. But I do feel that I must offer a word of warning and it is also essential that I go on to speak of an alternative path.

First, the word of warning. I remember a soldier of the Second World War telling me what a relief it was when he was captured in the North African desert. For him the war was over. He was in the hands of his captors and for the rest of the war he was their responsibility. I have felt the same kind of relief when I have had to go to hospital for an operation. My life was in other people's hands and I could quietly leave it there. I had no responsibility save the passive one of being as co-operative as I possibly could.

When you surrender your life into the hands of a Saviour, that is what happens. You are relinquishing your own personal responsibility for your life. From that moment onwards you belong to your Saviour and it is your Saviour who will dictate the future course of your life – a course which may be pretty much the same as it has always been but which may be radically different.

The trouble is, it won't actually be your Saviour who determines your future. When you surrender to enemy troops they pass you on and you end up in the hands of prison guards (or at least, that is what is supposed to happen). When you surrender to a Saviour you actually end up being directed by servants of that Saviour.

They may well be very fine people. They may well be highly trained experts in their field with wide experience. They may well do their very best for you and you may find that placing yourself in their hands is the best thing you have ever done. You may well find that your life is transformed for good.

But the simple fact is that these servants of your Saviour are still people. So they will make mistakes. And sometimes they will look at someone in their hands and have to acknowledge that they haven't a clue what to do with him. If you end up by becoming one of their mistakes; or if you end up in the no man's wilderness of their confusion; you could find yourself right back where you started from – in a real mess.

There is also another more sinister danger when people begin surrendering their lives into the hands of a god or a saviour. There are a few 'servants of god' who have quite dreadful ideas of what their god requires. Those who surrender their lives can find themselves involved in the ultimate sacrifice of suicide bombing – which is only one of the perversions surrender can lead to.

I grew up with the concept of surrender and was frequently called to make that surrender. When I joined the Christian ministry I placed my life in the hands of Jesus and his church. In practical terms, of course, that means his church.

When I faced my own personal tsunami I was in my early forties and I fully expected that I would take that path of surrender again. All of my training and all of my background suggested that that is the way I would go. But it was not long before I began to realise that there was another path which was beckoning to me. I began to find that my path demanded that I stand upon my own feet and that I take back my own personal responsibility for my life.

After a tsunami people wander in the desolate wilderness that has been their home. They feel utterly lost. They cling to tiny, pathetic reminders of the past. But little by little the will to live again returns. They begin to put down markers of their new life and their new home. Slowly, very slowly, energy returns and there is a hint of determination and even hope.

Although mercifully the mind has the power to blot out a great deal from the past, the fact that there was a past is not forgotten. The tsunami we created for ourselves is not forgotten and the havoc it wrought in lives other than our own is not forgotten. But step by step and brick by brick a new life is built.

It is built on personal responsibility. It is built on the foundation of an ethical system chosen now, not because it was the system we were taught, but because it holds the values and the goals which have become our own values and goals.

There is always the awareness that we are vulnerable and that our passions can bring us crashing down again. But that means that we are perhaps more on our guard than we were in the past.

The years slip by and with age those passions weaken or

they lose their power because they have been overtaken by another greater new passion in our lives. We are never again so foolish as to believe that we are invulnerable or invincible but, as the body weakens, we do feel stronger and stronger in the fundamentals of our lives.

After the tsunami we learn that all is not lost. We can begin again. We can play the game of life all over again. We can, in considerable measure, live our lives so that we can hold our heads up. And yes, we can find that deep content which is true happiness.

The religious path of total surrender begins in the solitary surrender of the worshipper to the Saviour. But it cannot continue without the support of the religious family, the community to which the worshipper belongs.

The path of personal responsibility also begins utterly alone. Is any one of us strong enough to continue alone?

My own journey would not have been possible without my parents and my family – especially my parents and my children. And then came 'good friends, friends whose arms held me up when my strength let me down.' And then, and forever since, my second wife Wendy. If we choose to stand alone it is not long before we discover that without love and friendship we are lost. But love and friendship can sustain us through the darkest days and make life wonderful again.

Ethics suffers from another inadequacy which I have not touched on at all. I have spoken throughout this chapter as if life is always a question of right or wrong, black or white. It isn't. There are many, many times when we are faced with choices between different 'goods' or even between the greater or lesser 'of two evils'. Choice in life is often not simple. Ethics may help us to make our choices; a religion or set of rules may tell us what to do but will not necessarily get it right. In the end, we are on our own and we have to make our own choices and live with them. As we live with them and rise above our immediate situation, the fog of uncertainty clears and we begin to find our way forward once more.

20

Where Do We Go From Here?

I suppose we could begin by looking back over the last two thousand years! Haven't there been any circular thinkers in all of that time? Yes, of course, but because their thinking IS circular they haven't really come up with much that is new and a great deal of what they have been doing is simply a re-examination of the ideas I have outlined so far.

Religion makes that abundantly clear. There hasn't been a *major* new religion since the birth of Islam, and the next youngest is Christianity. So virtually all religious thinking is still derived from ancient times. With the exception of Marxist Communism, pretty much the same thing can be said of irreligious thinking. The socialist ideals behind Communism captivated many people in the generation before mine and to a lesser degree, captivated my own generation, and even for a time inspired the best I have ever known in British political life before greed and self-interest returned to domination. Perhaps Marxism deserves to be looked at more thoroughly, but I don't feel competent to look at it.

While circular thinkers have been running around in circles, straight line thinkers have transformed the world in which we live. School-friends of mine whose parents were farmers spent hours discussing the merits and demerits of the very first tractors their farms had ever seen and, of course, all of them still had working horses. Now look at farming!

Similarly, the kitchen of my childhood bears very little resemblance to the kitchen of today. Some years ago I took a 16 year old to the Science Museum in Kensington and saw things there that we had used when I was a boy at home. . . in a MUSEUM!

Sitting typing (yes, grandchildren I know I should have a computer) in my centrally heated house, warmly clothed, well fed, with my own in-house entertainment and with my own car outside, life seems pretty good. Straight-line thinkers have achieved all this for us.

But sadly, that is not the whole story. To achieve what has been achieved there have been centuries of massive human degradation and suffering; there have been extinctions of large numbers of other creatures; and we are now reaching the point where the earth's resources are beginning to run out. Everyone knows about oil but perhaps much more serious than that is our over-use of water. The prophets of doom see us on our driverless bus running ever faster towards our own extinction.

Right or wrong? It seems to me that extinction may ultimately be an inevitable end of living on this planet, but there are still humans who have the supreme self-confidence that assures us that every problem can be solved and if it throws up new problems, they can be solved too.

Yet how do we solve the problem of man's inhumanity

to man? I switch on my in-house entertainment, my TV, and I see men and women blowing one another to bits, poisoning one another, driving one another out of their homes and countries. And all of this is done in the name of religion or political systems like democracy. It is all an expression of the human lust for power and wealth, or an expression of human hatreds and enmities that go back hundreds of years. If this is the way humans behave then they deserve to become extinct.

It is those same straight-line thinkers who have made life so good for so many of us, who have developed ever more dreadful means of making life terrible too.

It all makes you wonder whether there is any value or point in all of the circular thinking which has been my focus. Is there any point at all in decent people, religious or irreligious, trying their very best to examine how best life should be lived when some of their fellow humans live so foully and destructively?

If there isn't, then my last 80 years have been a complete waste of time!

I grew up during the Second World War. Even at such a time as that, when millions upon millions of people were killed and millions upon millions more suffered more grievously than I can begin to describe – even then, and in some ways perhaps, especially then, you could still say of most of the people of the world what that Taoist said so long ago: most people are kind, decent, loving, straight-forward, honest, thoughtful and so on and so on.

My own pathway through life has taken me quite literally into the homes of thousands of people, from some of the most poverty stricken people in the world to some seriously wealthy people. In all of that, my experience of almost everyone I have met has chimed in with the words of that Taoist.

Is this the result of all of our circular thinking or is our circular thinking simply an exposition of the way people are? It is the question of the chicken and the egg all over again – another circular question for us to whittle over. Are people decent because of all the ideals we have set before them or are those ideals simply an expression of the decency which is natural in human beings? I'm afraid I haven't a clue, but if pressed I would say that the living comes first and the thinking follows. First we look at good lives and then we look at what comprises a good life.

But it does seem to me that after all of this 'running around in circles' we do tend to end up with ideals and goals which at rock bottom are pretty similar, and that is true whether we are religious or not. All of us seem to have similar concerns with what constitutes a good life and how best we should live that life. And as western life grows ever more individualistic perhaps we need those community based ethical systems more and more.

So many people today live on their own, far from the roots of the community where they were born. They have no husbands, wives, partners or children and they have left the bosom of the older generation. So perhaps it becomes increasingly important that they should be able to find a community where they can feel at ease with like-minded people. For some this will involve a religion, for others it won't. But whether within religion or outside it, we all need to find a route through life that is happy, fulfilling and satisfying.

I spent the first half of my life within a religion and I say to all of my readers who are still religious, 'Enjoy your

133

religion. Don't make a song and dance about it and don't feel that you have to ram it down the throats of everybody else, but enjoy it. Enjoy its sense of community; enjoy its discipline; and aim to be as fine a representative of your religion as you can be. That, after all, is YOUR way of becoming a thoroughly good and decent human being.'

I have spent the second half of my life outside religion, doing my best to serve those who, like me, have no religious beliefs or religious home. I say to my fellow unbelievers, 'enjoy your place in life. Don't make a song and dance about it and don't feel that you have to ram your views down the throats of everybody else, but enjoy them. Enjoy your own communities; 'Enjoy the discipline of thoughtful, ethical lives; and aim to be as fine a representative of unbelievers as you can be. That, after all, is YOUR way of becoming a thoroughly good and decent human being.'

And what is a thoroughly good and decent human being?

Have you ever seen pictures of penguins en masse in Antarctica trying to cope with the bitter cold by huddling together?

Imagine if those penguins were people. They would know that the warmest place to be is in the middle of the crowd with the warmth of others all around them. So they would be battling and burrowing hard to push their way in from the edges regardless of the other people they had to push out of their way. And all around the periphery of the crowd of people there would be those who have succumbed to the cold and died.

But penguins are not people. They are only a model of how people ought to be. That crowd of penguins looked from a distance to be quite still, but it wasn't. It was engaged in a kind of dance, a shuffle, shuffle here and a nudge, nudge there leading the whole community to be constantly on the move. And those on the outside find their way in and those on the inside find their way out in a never ending swapping of positions that ensures that no penguin is ever in the coldest spots for too long. The dance is one of caring for one another which ensures that they all survive the hazards of life.

My other favourite picture also comes from the world of the birds. My picture of the penguins might suggest that there is only one people and that there is only one dance. At its deepest level I believe that that is true. But few of us are ready to acknowledge that truth wholeheartedly. We still like to think of ourselves in separate compartments just as we think of sparrows, robins, blackbirds and so on as different kinds of birds.

And different kinds of birds have different kinds of dance, although it still often has a good deal to do with survival in a dangerous world. On the mud flats and estuaries of our rivers it is often possible to stand in wonder and watch as thousands of birds take to the air together, swirl around overhead and in due course, settle down again. Different birds have different styles – different dances.

The one with which I am most familiar is the incredible dance of massed starlings in flight. Millions of them fly in such harmony that they paint beautiful pictures in the air, merging and parting, swirling around and filling the sky before finally falling into the trees to a million and more perches for the night. How on earth do they do it? You never see them bump into one another or crash. It seems impossible.

I'm sorry to come down from these ethereal heights but it seems that there are students who have tried to work out how they do manage it. I don't remember their university: Norwich, Nottingham, Leicester? They claim that each starling relates to the seven starlings nearest to it and that that enables them to fly in such a marvellous way together.

Many years ago I read that at any given time most human beings will be in some sort of a relationship with about one hundred and twenty others. I've never sat down and tried to work out how true that is either of me or of anybody else. Add or subtract any number you like to think of, until it becomes true for you.

Just imagine what human life would be like if every one of us could emulate the starlings and relate harmoniously with all of those one hundred and twenty – more or less. Imagine if I could do it. Imagine if my children could do it. Their one hundred and twenties overlap with mine but they are not the same as mine, so the flock is beginning to grow. Imagine if you could do it, and go on imagining.

It seems to me that in the penguins and the starlings we have two pictures which gather together all the hopes and dreams of all the best of us offering a world where we can learn to live in peace and harmony with one another, striving very simply just to be the best that we can be. In the end, that is what all the circular thinking in the world, of every age, is looking for.